M000191851

CONTENTS

CONTENTS

THE ENSEMBLE STUDIO THEATRE

Marathon '84

357 W. 20th STREET, NYC, NY 10011

ENSEMBLE STUDIO THEATRE, MARATHON '84

First printing: August 1985

ISBN: 0-88145-030-8

Design by Marie Donovan
Set in Baskerville by L&F Technical Composition, Lakeland, FL
Printed and bound by The Whitlock Press, Middletown, NY

The Ensemble Studio Theatre was founded in 1971 by Curt Dempster as a membership organization of playwrights, actors, directors, designers, and technicians. Over the past 14 years the original membership of 20 has grown to include more than 300, and the theatre has expanded to include an Institute for Professional Training, a Playwrights Unit, a Summer Theatre Conference, and a Los Angeles branch. Mr. Dempster, who has served as the theatre's Artistic Director since its inception, describes The Ensemble as "... an ecological cause—not just theatre, but a daily struggle to create new plays and keep them alive in an increasingly hostile environment."

From the beginning the emphasis has been on *process—whether in the writing of a play or in the creation of a role—rather than product*. The needs of the individual work determine the method and manner of its development. Most of the works produced on the Mainstage have gone through several stages of development including readings, staged readings, and workshops. The Mainstage season includes: four full-length plays; *Octoberfest*, The Ensemble's month-long festival of member-initiated projects; the *Music Theatre Workshop*, staged readings of new musical works; *New Voices*, a series of staged readings of new American plays; and the annual *Marathon*, the Ensemble's spring festival of new one-act plays. In addition to the Mainstage season, the theatre develops over 200 new scripts annually. Many of these are member-initiated workshops in which members often choose to explore other disciplines: actors write, designers perform, technicians direct.

With the success of these various work-in-progress programs, The Ensemble provides a unique and necessary service to both the New York theatre and the American theatre at large. It has become one of the leading developmental theatres in the country and it continues to present new work by established playwrights and acts as a breeding ground for talented newcomers. The *One-Act Marathon* is now one of the New York theatre season's most anticipated events and is responsible for bringing plays such as Christopher Durang's *Sister Mary Ignatius Explains It All for You*, Marsha Norman's *The Laundromat*, Michael Weller's *Split*, Shirley Lauro's *Open Admissions*, and Shel Silverstein's *The Lady Or the Tiger* to public attention.

The theatre is the recipient of many awards, including:

- The Outer Critics' Circle Award for "outstanding contribution to the American theatre."
- Several Obie awards
- The American Theatre Wing Commendation—1982
- *The New York Times* Best Theatrical Achievement Award—1981 and 1982
- The National Endowment for the Arts Three-Year Advancement Grant

Playwright-members have been recognized for their individual work by the National Endowment for the Arts, The Rockefeller Foundation, the Creative Arts Public Service Award, the Guggenheim Fellowship, the Academy Awards, and the Pulitzer Prize.

DAVID MAMET

DAVID MAMET is a Ensemble Studio Theatre member playwright whose works include *Shoeshine, A Sermon, Five Unrelated Pieces, The Frog Prince* (all produced at the Ensemble), *Edmond, American Buffalo, Sexual Perversity in Chicago, The Woods,* and *Lakeboat.* Mr. Mamet was nominated for an Academy Award for his screenplay of *The Verdict. Glengarry Glen Ross* had a successful run at the National Theatre in London and on Broadway, and was awarded the Pulitzer Prize in 1984. In Chicago, Mr. Mamet's adaptation of *The Cherry Orchard* inaugurated the New Theatre Company's first season, followed by their productions of his one-acts *The Shawl* and *The Spanish Prisoner. Warm and Cold,* was published in the spring of 1985.

The following four *Vermont Sketches—Conversations with the Spirit World, Pint's a Pound the World Around, Dowsing,* and *Deer Dogs*—were first presented at the Marathon '84 festival of One-Act Plays on May 24 with the following cast under the direction of Gregory Mosher:

Conversations:
Frank Hamilton   Colin Stinton

Pint's a Pound:
W.H. Macy   Joe Ponazecki

Dowsing:
Frank Hamilton   Joe Ponazecki

Deer Dogs:
W.H. Macy   Colin Stinton

For Stock and amateur production rights, contact: Samuel French, Inc., 45 West 25th Street, New York, NY 10011. For all other rights, contact: Rosenstone/Wender, 3 East 48th Street, New York, NY 10017.

CONVERSATIONS WITH THE SPIRIT WORLD

Characters

MORRIS
JAMES

MORRIS: Dowsing for the like the kid says, "What cha doin'?" Says, "I'm *dowsing.*" "What is that?" "I'm looking for this *line* ... "Line is *that*?" ... "Line I'm *looking* for ..." He points. "That *purple* line ...?"

JAMES: No ...

MORRIS: *Yes,* and by damn if he didn't point it *out.*

JAMES: He *saw* it?

MORRIS: Well, that's what I'm *telling* you ... "What are you doing?" "Dowsing for a *well* ... " By god, I'm trine to get these silly *sticks* to work ...

JAMES: ... Uh-huh ...

MORRIS: S'I find this *line,* I'm trying to feel the line and Clark can *see* ... I'll tell you something else: *Ivers.*

JAMES: Now who is that ...?

MORRIS: Say eighteen *thirty* ... say eighteen, to eighteen forty-*five, fifty, hired* man up to Hayes place ...

JAMES: Uh-huh ...

MORRIS: ... he died, *Clara* said that he didn't go *over.*

JAMES: ... old *Hayes* farm ...

MORRIS: The old *Hayes* farm. The *hired* man. Now: Annie, she was *young,* you know, we'd hear her *talking* ...

JAMES: ... Uh-huh ...

MORRIS: ... young folks do, a little kid, you know, a year old, she'd be *talking* ...

JAMES: She'd be talking to herself ...

MORRIS: Uh-huh ... one day. we're up there, Clara asks her who she's *talking* to. She says, "This man ..."

JAMES: Uh-huh.

MORRIS: So she ... now, I think, *I think* what Annie says is *Clara* asks her, "What's his name?" Annie says "Ivan," something like that. Later it occurs to me, now where'd she get *that* from ...?

JAMES: The Russians.

MORRIS: ... What *I* thought. But even *so*, something she *heard*? Where would she *hear* that. I told ... I remember this, I'm telling stories on my *kids* ...

JAMES: ... Uh-huh ...

MORRIS: To *Chunk*, I think it was ...

JAMES: Chunk *Kellog*.

MORRIS: Yes. Said, "Where she *gets* it from ... some man named *Ivan*." He said, "Ask her was it Ivan she said or *Ivers*." Who he was, as I said, a *hired* man, a hundred years ago.

JAMES: He die a violent death?

MORRIS: I don't *know*. What *Chunk* said ... *yes*. *Yes*. I think he did. He, what *Chunk* said, he didn't want to go *across* ...

JAMES: Uh-huh ...

MORRIS: And, to that *time* he habited the house.

JAMES: Annie remember this?

MORRIS: Well, you don't *know* ...

JAMES: Uh-huh ...

MORRIS: Whether she, what she *saw*, or the *stories* ...

JAMES: ... Uh-huh ...

MORRIS: ... you know ...

JAMES: Yes.

MORRIS: ... that she remembers that we'd tell. And she *described* him.

JAMES: What'd she say?

MORRIS: A man, you know, I don't remember ... *beard*

JAMES: ... Uh-huh ...

MORRIS: A heavy *shirt* ...

JAMES: Mm. (*Pause*)

MORRIS: Reason *I thought* of it, dowsing for water, and *Clark* says ...

JAMES: Well, they say ninety percent *anyone* can dowse ...

MORRIS: ... that's right ...

JAMES: ... and a *hundred* percent all *children*.

MORRIS: That's right. (*Pause*) That's right.

JAMES: *Jean* saw something out on the hill.

MORRIS: What was that?

JAMES: ... the old *sugar* lane ...?

MORRIS: Uh-huh ...

JAMES: *Dusk* one day ...

MORRIS: When was this?

JAMES: Last fall.

MORRIS: Uh-huh.

JAMES: She got me, I was in the *bedroom*, she comes in ...

MORRIS: What was it ...?

JAMES: She says, "A boy." (*Pause*) A boy? "Out at the entrance to the lane." "Now, who would *that* be ...?" I could

tell, it was *something* she saw. I said, "A deer." "No."
"Waal, you know, they put that white tail up ..."

MORRIS: ... Uh-huh ...

JAMES: She says, "No, No, It wasn't a *deer*." (*Pause*) "It
was a boy." She said she *felt* something, you know, like you
do ...

MORRIS: Mm ...

JAMES: ... she looked *around* ...

MORRIS: Where was she?

JAMES: On the porch ...

MORRIS: Mm.

JAMES: There was a *boy*. He *saw* her, and he ran up the lane.
(*Pause*) Now: (*Pause*) where would he be *coming* from ...?

MORRIS: ... I don't know.

JAMES: Well, I don't know *either*. Nothing up there, and
what would he be *doing* up there ...? (*Pause*)

MORRIS: Now when was this?

JAMES: Just at dusk. I said, "You see funny things in that
light." (*Pause*) "Yes, she says," "I saw this plain as day,
though, and it was a *boy*. He *saw* me, and he ran away."

MORRIS: Did she say what he was wearing?

JAMES: No, and I'll tell you, I didn't want to *press* her.
(*Pause*)

MORRIS: Uh-huh.

JAMES: ... 'cause she was growing frightened. (*Pause*)

MORRIS: She'd *seen* something.

JAMES: Mm.

MORRIS: You know what it was?

JAMES: No, I don't. (*Pause*) No.

MORRIS: Mm.

JAMES: I know there's places in the woods where I don't like to go ...

MORRIS: Mm. (*Pause*) There's places I don't like to go *either*. (*Pause*)

JAMES: *You* don't ...

MORRIS: (*Pause*) No. (*Pause*)

JAMES: Mm.

PINT'S A POUND THE WORLD AROUND

A: ... don't have the twelve-inch. We have the ten-inch and the fourteen-inch.

B: Isn't that always the way?

A: Seems it is. A number two do?

B: No.

A: Allright. The guy should have been in *Tuesday*, I 'spect him *Friday*, if he don't come then ... I'll tell you, I've been thinking of switching. 'Merican *United*, I can get twenty percent over a year, you sign on to their Ownership Subscriber Plan, you get a basis of twenty percent, you want something it's *there*. The next day. Six days.

B: Where they out of?

A: Down in Manchester. *Basis* of twenty percent, they've got a *newspaper*, what do you call it, a *flyer*, the *specials*, they can go, sometimes they beat the Marketway sixty percent.

B: No.

A: Absolutely.

B: How's the quality?

A: Same, better. Most things better, much of ... what they *do*. *You* know, they've got their *brand* ...

B: Uh-huh ...

A: *Good* stuff. Heavy gauge stuff, Some of ... *you* know their stuff ...

B: ... sure ...

A: ... same patterns eighteen ninety-eight ...

B: When's that, when they got started?

A: When they got started. Yes. Fellow name of ... I had the guy in here, I was looking at their stuff since I came in. You have to sign *up*, what you do, you buy stock in the *company*, the minimum buy-in thirty-two hundred dollars, you own *stock*, at the end of the year they go and *prorate* you the amount of your sales, and you're discounted based on that.

B: And what do you do with the discount?

A: What do you do?

B: What, do you apply it to your ...

A: Well, I guess you do. I never thought of it. I suppose that you ... or you could take it in cash. I had the guy here just the other day.

B: They want you to sign up.

A: The closest, *"Jim's"*, in *Bradenburg's* American ...

B: He is ...

A: Oh yeah. You see his prices in there? Beat the *Marketway* fifteen percent *easily*. On *everthing*. He *has* to ...

B: They spend their money on advertising.

A: That's what I'm *saying*. It ain't going in the *stock*, in stock improvement ... dealer *relations* ... it's going in the *television* ads. Schiff, started eighteen ninety-eight. American United, the whole operation's built on one thing: the relation with the *dealers*.

B: Mm.

A: Stockholders are the dealer, *customers* the dealer. Everything. Geared toward one man. I pick up the phone, I say, "Where are the ... *whatever*, he said that they'd be here on *Thursday*." Marketway, what do *they* care ...? No *displays*, very few *incentives* ... like I'm buying *retail* from them. You complain to someone, their attitude, basically, I think, I don't think they do it on *purpose*, but what you get is: if you don't want the franchise, you can turn back. They don't care. What they think, they're doing you a *favor*, all the money they've spent on the TV ads. Some stores, maybe,

though I doubt it. Not in *here*. A fella comes in here he wants
three of those, four of those, something he broke on a job, he
wants it this afternoon: *I'm built on service.* He goes down the
road, he can go to the *Star* supply in *Worth*, he's in the habit
to come here, I want to *keep* him here. Two things they told
me: Never change your hours, never cut your stock.

B: Uh-huh.

A: A fellow comes by some hour you've 'spose to be open
and you're *closed*, next time he thinks heavily 'fore he drives
out of his way. "Maybe he's closed ..."

B: That's very true.

A: ... it makes no difference it only happened one time. It's
like adultery. I'm not foolin you. He thinks, "It happened
once, it could happen again."

B: Uh-huh.

A: Fellow comes in here, something he needs on a job, he
needs it this afternoon, I'm *out* of it, what does he think?
"Shit, I could of drove the same distance to *Star* and had it,
and probably *cheaper* ..." Something else. If I can get with
the *American*, I'm going to beat Marketway, I'm going to
beat *Star*. I'm going to have them coming *here* from Worth ...

B: You think?

A: There's no two ways about it. I'll have the stock, I'll have
the variety, I'll have *quality*. ... They marshal their *franchises
very* careful. Forty-two miles to Brandenburgs, the closest
they could have another is here. I've got no competition. I'll
have them coming in from Worth, from *Peacham* ...

B: And it's just the down payment ...

A: What it is, yes, it's a down payment, it's an *investment*,
you're actually buying stock. Whatever it is, I looked it up a
week ago, a couple of weeks ago, seventeen dollars a share.
What is that? Two into thirty-five, two shares for thirty-five,
two hundred shares, thirty-five hundred dollars. Which you
earn in the dividend on, too, whatever that is ...

B: On the stock.

A: Yes.

B: You should go with them.

A: I *would*. I *would* and I think I will. I think June and I have almost decided to *go* with them. It's a big step, but I think it's
worth it. That's what I think. Many things. You have to look
down the road. It's a big step now, it's a big *investment*, it's a *com-
mitment*, in certain ways it would mean taking on more *stock*. ...

B: Why is that?

A: Well, you have a basic *order*. Whatever your *size* is: the
classification that they give you ... on your *footage* ... on your
overhead ... then when you order you have a minimum order
that you have to file. (*Pause*) You also have a minimum order
per *month* ... they come in and they do the inventory ...

B: *They* do.

A: Yep. They do. At the end of the year ... I think that that's
a good idea. They come in, a team, ten people, something,
calculators, they're out in an afternoon, they come in Sunday afternoon ... whenever you're closed, they work through
the night, they're out Monday morning. *That's* a good idea
... you ever do an inventory?

B: No.

A: Hell on Earth. I worked in a shoestore once. I thought I
was going to go mad. ... But it's a big step. (*Pause*)

B: Mm.

A: (*Pause*) It's a big step. (*Pause*)

B: *Well——*

A: Yeaaah! Five of the Number three. Twelve-inch. I'm
almost sure I'll have them Friday.

B: I'll be back.

A: I'm going to call him again today. I would say ninety percent. Ninety-five percent. I'll have them Friday. I'll tell you:

If he *doesn't* come in, I'm going to be down in Worth, Friday night, if he *doesn't* come in, I'll pick them up, you stop in Saturday morning ...

B: *That's* okay ...

A: No. I should *have* 'em. No trouble at all. You come in Friday, he hasn't stopped in, I'll have 'em Saturday first thing.

B: That's all right.

A: No trouble at all. I'm sorry I don't *have* 'em. I *should*. It doesn't help *you* to tell you that the *man* didn't come in.

B: Well, *thank* you.

A: That's all right. You take care, now.

B: You, too.

A: It's nice talking to you.

DOWSING

(Setting: Two older men in a Vermont country store.)

A: *Yessuh.* Fella told me he said, "I don't want no more of them *dowsers* in here." By garry, I said, he's got a thing or two to learn.

B: I *guess* ...

A: I said to you, Jim, *you're* a Mason, I said you did something I don't like, "I don't want no more *Masons* in here ...

B: No. Mason's supposed t'believe in brotherhood.

A: Yes. But if I told *you* something you did, I'se going to, you know, take it *out* on ...

B: Yuh.

A: ... on other *Masons* ...

B: Well, I'd say that's *foolish.*

A: ... What *I'd* say.

B: You say he didn't want the *dowsers?*

A: *Dowsers* were down to his place ...

B: ... Uh-huh ...

A: Some woman called, she wanted to know was her *friend* there, he says, "She's your friend, you should *know* if she's here." She called the chamber of *commerce,* he gets this *complaint,* the fella calls him up he says, "By garry, *keep* 'em!" says he'll do without 'em. Big mistake. One week of the year that they're here, he's *booked,* you know, they come spend their *money* ...

B: ... Uh-huh ...

A: *They* don't care it cost twenty-five dollars, thirty-five, they don't care, they're, you know ...

B: Um hmm ...

A: Well, they're on vacation. Any business you meet some you'd rather not *deal* with. I think he's a *fool*.

B: Now: (*Pause*) When you say "dowsin'"—is that the same dowsin' that we use to do with a bent stick?

A: It is.

B: For *water*.

A: Well, they dowse for *water*, dowse for *oil* ...

B: For *oil* ...?

A: For oil in the ground. Yessuh.

B: ... that a fact ...

A: It is. For ... well, you know, they might, say, you know, if they wanted to lay out a *field*, what to put where ...

B: ... yuh ...

A: ... in what corner of the *field* ...

B: ... Uh-huh ...

A: They'd dowse for that.

B: And how'd they find it?

A: Little *string*, a *weight* on it, they dowse it, yes or no. (*Pause*) Eh? They ask the *question*, string moves *one* way, then it's "yes." The other way is "no."

B: The way it *rotates*.

A: *Yessir*.

B: You know, I could never ... fellas take that *stick* ... you know, I took it, never did a thing, just laid there in my hand. Other man took it, twisted every *which* way ...

A: I know.

B: Never did a *thing* for me.

A: Me, either. (*Pause*)

B: And that is their *convention*. Is that the thing?

A: Yup. Up *Morristown. You* know that.

B: Yup.

A: Yuh.

B: Up to *Morristown*.

A: Yuh. (*Pause*)

B: I heard it's going to frost tonight.

A: They had a fellow, Connie *Barr* ...

B: Yuh.

A: You remember Connie?

B: Yes, I do.

A: His sister lost her watch, he found it with a dowsing stick.

B: Who was his sister?

A: Eunice Craft.

B: The *Craft* girls ...?

A: No. She married Billy Craft.

B: She *married* Billy.

A: Yessir.

B: D'I know her?

A: I think you did.

B: Mm.

A: Lost her watch, he found it.

B: With a dowsing stick?

A: Uh huh.

B: Where was it.

A: In the field.

B: In plain sight?

A: I don't *think* so. 'Cause she'd lost it for a month.

B: She had?

A: Yeh.

B: And he found it?

A: Yes. He did.

B: Most like he *put* it there.

A: Well, that's what we thought at the *time*, but he held out he found it dowsing.

B: How about that now.

A: And I think that he *did*.

B: Well, you know, the things that you *see*, it makes you think that maybe there's something to *everything*.

A: Now, by God, that's the truth.

B: Mm?

A: *Yessir*.

B: *Ayuh*.

DEER DOGS

(*Two men*, LARRY *and* BUNCHY, *are at a country store. There are also a couple of onlookers.*)

LARRY: Dog's runnin' deer it should be shot.

BUNCHY: But who's to tell it's runnin' deer? *Law* says you see a dog in pursuit of a deer you can *shoot* him. Who's to say it's ... wait, wait, you take *Dave* here: Keeps his dog tied up. One day th' dog, say Larry *Thompson's* dog, is running by— *Dave's* dog gets loose. ... Larry's dog's runnin' deer. Someone sees it and, down the road later on, Larry's dog *and* Dave's dog. What does he do? Shoot 'em both.

LARRY: How did Dave's dog get loose?

BUNCHY: ... I'm saying a dog which is *usually* tied down, *Dave's* dog ...

LARRY: How did it get loose?

BUNCHY: I'm saying one day when it *is* loose ... I don't *know* how it got loose ...

LARRY: And was it runnin' deer ...?

BUNCHY: No.

LARRY: How do you know?

BUNCHY: 'Cause it hasn't got a *taste* for them. It's a tame dog.

LARRY: How do you know?

BUNCHY: Well, now, now, now, because it *is* a tame dog: I, you *know* that dog ...

LARRY: ... I'm ...

BUNCHY: ... *I* know what you're ...

LARRY: I'm ...

BUNCHY: I know what you're, wait a second—I know what you're saying ... that the dog is, *though* the dog is tame, it gets loose it starts runnin deer. Is that it?

LARRY: Yes.

BUNCHY: But what I'm saying, this case we *know* that the dog is tame. It's tame. It *isn't* runnin' deer. All right? It's DAVE'S DOG. It's *tame*. It's been tied up constantly ...

LARRY: How does it ...

BUNCHY: ... that's not ...

LARRY: ... how does it get loose?

BUNCHY: Well, say that Dave forgot to tie it up.

LARRY: And where does it go?

BUNCHY: ... I ...

LARRY: Where does it go?

BUNCHY: I know what you're saying. It goes to the woods. All right.

LARRY: What is it doing there?

BUNCHY: It's *out*. With Larry Thompson's dog.

LARRY: What are they doing?

BUNCHY: *Larry's* dog is runnin' deer.

LARRY: And what is Dave's dog doing?

BUNCHY: I don't know.

LARRY: Well, I don't know *either*—but *I'm* going to assume it's runnin' deer. (*Pause*)

BUNCHY: Would you shoot it?

LARRY: Yes, I would.

BUNCHY: You'd shoot Dave's dog?

LARRY: Yes. I would. (*Pause*)

BUNCHY: (*Snorts*) You would shoot Dave's dog? (*Pause*)

LARRY: Yes. I would.

BUNCHY: Because you know that *that's* the dog that'll be caught. Not Larry *Thompson's* dog. (*Pause*) *That's* the dog that will be caught ... *Shoot*. It's a bad law ... I'm sorry. (*Pause*) I don't like it.

LARRY: You'll like it when you go out in the woods there ain't no *deer* ...

BUNCHY: (*Pause*) *Nossir*. (*Pause*) No *sir* ... N' I'm going to tell you one more thing: What the *Law* ... wait a second—what the law *encourages* a fella to do is—I'm not saying *you* or *me*, but what it sets a man up to do is to say, "I'm going to shoot that fella's *dog*." That's not right. (*Pause*)

BILL BOZZONE

BILL BOZZONE was born in Brooklyn, New York. His plays, including *Saxophone Music, Buck Fever,* and *Touch Black,* have been produced Off-off Broadway at the Ensemble Studio Theatre and regionally at the Philadelphia Festival Theatre, the Playwrights Lab of Minneapolis, and the Daytona Playhouse.

A recipient of a National Endowment for the Arts Fellowship in Playwriting in 1984, Mr. Bozzone also has received fellowships and grants from the Atlantic Center for the Arts (where he worked with Edward Albee), the Dutchess County Arts Council, and CAPS.

An adjunct instructor in English at Marist College, in Poughkeepsie, New York, Bill Bozzone currently resides in Dutchess County, New York with writer/wife Tricia Bauer.

Saxophone Music was first presented at the Marathon '84 Festival of One-Act Plays on May 26 with the following cast under the direction of Risa Bramon:

HECTOR: Ned Eisenberg   EMIL: David Strathairn
MARGO: Ilene Kristen   MRS. FIRESTONE: Mary Davenport

Scenery was by Jane Musky; lighting by Karl E. Hass; sound by Bruce Ellman; costumes by Linda Vigdor; live saxophone solos by Louis Belogenis. Denise A. Laffer was the production stage manager, and Mark Gordon the assistant director.

For Stock and amateur production rights, contact: Broadway Play Publishing, 357 W. 20th Street., New York, New York 10011. For all other rights, contact: Rosenstone/ Wender, 3 East 48th Street, New York, NY 10017.

SAXOPHONE MUSIC

For

Tricia Bauer

and

Edward Albee

Scene One

(TIME: *Tuesday. Late fall. Early evening.* SCENE: *A room in a New York City boarding hotel. One door at left. A double bed center. Two straight-backed chairs, one right center and the other left center. A large window up right center and a standing lamp controlled by a wall switch near the door. An old wooden dresser with mirror down right center. A worn rug.*)

(*At rise, darkness. The voice of* MRS. FIRESTONE *calls from downstairs: SHADDUP BEFORE I SEND SOMEBODY UP THERE TO SHUT YOU UP!! A saxophone plays, low at first, something upbeat—a jazz version of* "Sunny Side of the Street" *perhaps. A few bars into the music:*)

HECTOR: Knock it off. (*The music continues.*) Knock it off!

(*Lights up full.* EMIL *stands near left center chair, the saxophone silent but still close to his lips.* EMIL *is in his late thirties, but bad hygiene makes him appear older. He is carelessly dressed and his shirt hangs half out. A brightly colored but dirty ski jacket hangs across the back of his (left center) chair. A closed saxophone case is on the seat of the chair.*)

(*By the open door, after just entering, is* HECTOR DIAZ. HECTOR *is 30, still relatively youthful. He wears a brown leather jacket and manages to keep himself surprisingly well groomed.*)

HECTOR: You give me a headache with that shit, man.

EMIL: I just thought a little music might——

(*As* HECTOR *speaks,* EMIL *closes the door, takes* HECTOR'S *jacket, and hangs it across the other chair.*)

HECTOR: Whole world screamin' in my ear all day. Now I come back here and listen to you on that thing. You know what you sound like? Two buffalos fucking. That's what you sound like.

(*Pause*)

EMIL: So how was your day?

HECTOR: How was my day. (*Beat*) How the fuck do you think? (*Pause.* HECTOR *goes to the window, looks out.*) (*Almost an apology*) Shit. (*Pause*) There's no heart out there, Emil. No heart, no soul, no jobs, nothing. Nobody listens, nobody fuckin' cares.

EMIL: You told them about your army training?

HECTOR: My army training I can stick right up my "culu." (HECTOR *turns from the window, goes to the saxophone case, puts it on the bed.*) Hey, but don't sweat it, baby. The cream always goes to the top.

EMIL: (*Approaching*) What are you doing?

HECTOR: (*Opening the case*) I'm taking five bucks, man. (EMIL, *firmly but politely, takes the case, closes it, "keeps" it.*)

EMIL: I'm handling the money, Hector. Remember? You promised.

HECTOR: I ain't ate all day!

EMIL: We only got 37 dollars left.

HECTOR: I just want a bite!

EMIL: Twelve forty for the train, $85 for one week's rent, $9 food and cosmetics—leaves us only $37 and some change.

HECTOR: Well what the hell am I supposed to do? Starve?

EMIL: Maybe I could get a job.

(*No response from* HECTOR.)

I washed dishes at "the chateau." I never broke one.

HECTOR: Well this is New York City, Emil. This ain't no group home.

EMIL: I know that.

HECTOR: Even the dishwashers out there got to be very ...

EMIL: Very what?

HECTOR: Very familiar with things. (*Short pause*) Somebody like you walking around ...

EMIL: What do you mean, "somebody like me?"

HECTOR: You know.

EMIL: (*Almost a challenge*) I'm stupid?

HECTOR: No.

EMIL: What?

(*Pause*)

HECTOR: You got no "street smarts," man. You don't read so good, you don't know how to get around, you don't communicate with people ...

EMIL: I could try.

HECTOR: Look at you. You can't even dress good. (*Short pause*) There's more to it than just blowing sweet on that fuckin' thing all day. C'mere.

(EMIL, *the sax in one hand and the case in the other, approaches.* HECTOR *tucks in* EMIL'S *shirt.*)

You remember how it was back in the place? It was me looking out for you and you doing stuff for me. Some of them creeps back there gave you trouble, who helped you out?

EMIL: You.

HECTOR: I needed a cigarette, somebody to change the channels on the TV ...

EMIL: Me.

HECTOR: Well that's how it was and that's how it's got to be.

EMIL: No dishwashing job?

HECTOR: No dishwashing job. Now gimme the five. (HEC-TOR *goes to the bed, opens the case, puts the saxophone in the case, closes the case.*)

EMIL: (*After a moment*) Maybe I was better off at "the chateau."

HECTOR: Yeah. With people throwing up in the floor. People sleeping all over the stairs. Shit. Gimme the five.

EMIL: The landlady yells when I play the saxophone here.

HECTOR: Hey, fuck that landlady. She ain't God. (*Short pause*) Besides, it's just temporary here. I told you. Soon as I get a job we find something better.

EMIL: At least at "the chateau" I could play my saxophone.

HECTOR: You can play the damn thing, Emil! Anytime you want! Just not now! (*Pause*) And don't hand me that bullshit about how you could play at "the chateau." You use to pull that thing out, everybody start screamin'. Fuckin' buncha animals with no musical appreciation. (*Short pause*) But, hey. Don't listen to me. You want to go, go. You want to spend your life in some "casa de locos ..."

EMIL: Cass what?

HECTOR: Crazy house, Emil.

EMIL: Hospital.

HECTOR: (*After a moment*) Hospital, huh? (*Short pause*) The sign outside by the parking lot say "hospital," huh? (*No response*) Sign say "Department of Mental Hygiene," Emil. Fancy words for crazy house.

EMIL: I don't belong in no crazy house.

(*No response from* HECTOR)

Down on my luck, maybe. They told me that. Just have to get back on my feet. That's all.

HECTOR: Well you never gonna get on anything up in that place, Emil. That place is for losers.

(*Pause*)

EMIL: You think they miss us?

HECTOR: Who cares. We got fifty miles on that place.

EMIL: I bet they miss their money.

HECTOR: Hey, it's part our money, too, man.

EMIL: Kind of makes me feel bad when I think of all that work down the drain.

HECTOR: So don't.

EMIL: The car wash, the craft sale, Monte Carlo night ...

HECTOR: I said, don't think about it!

EMIL: Everybody trusting me, making me treasurer, letting me hold the can ...

HECTOR: Get off it, Emil! You wanted to go as bad as me!

EMIL: Yeah, because you told me I could play the saxophone.

HECTOR: WELL PLAY THE FUCKIN' THING!

(*Pause*)

EMIL: I don't feel like playing it right now.

HECTOR: Then give me the five.

EMIL: No.

HECTOR: No?

EMIL: I can give you three.

HECTOR: Three?!

EMIL: We have to watch it. (EMIL *opens the case, takes out three singles, extends them.*)

HECTOR: (*After a moment*) You no longer do what I ask you to do?

(*No response*)

Emil, I take you with me because you do what I ask you to do. Not everybody will do what I ask them to do.

EMIL: I thought it was because we're friends.

HECTOR: Well don't push it.

(*Long pause.* EMIL *returns the singles, takes out a five, hands it to* HECTOR.)

(*Smiles*) You unreal, you know that? You worse than a fuckin' bank. What you eatin'? (*He puts on his jacket.*)

EMIL: Coffee and a hot dog.

HECTOR: With three bucks split in half, you'd be lucky to get the bun. (*He starts for the door.*)

EMIL: Hey, Hector?

(HECTOR *stops, faces him.*)

You wouldn't take off on me, would you?

HECTOR: Where am I gonna go on five bucks, Emil? (*He opens the door.*)

EMIL: Hector?

HECTOR: What?

EMIL: It's okay if I play the saxophone?

HECTOR: Hey, it's your house, man. You do what you want. (*He starts out the door.*)

EMIL: Hey, Hector!

HECTOR: What?!

EMIL: See ya.

BLACKOUT
Scene Two

(TIME: *The following afternoon.* HECTOR, *his shirt open, makes up the bed. In front of the mirror* MARGO, *a 40-year old prostitute, applies fresh lipstick.* MARGO'S *coat and bag are on the left center chair. The saxophone case is by the leg of that chair.*)

HECTOR: I bet you get a lotta guys ask you the same question. (*He stops making the bed, mocks a swinger.*) "How was it for you, baby?" You get a lotta guys like that?

MARGO: Sa.

HECTOR: What?

MARGO: (*Lowering lipstick*) I said, some.

HECTOR: Oh. (*He returns to making the bed. After a moment.*) So how *was* it for you?

MARGO: (*A poker face*) I saw stars.

HECTOR: (*Slight laugh*) Yeah. Sure you did.

(*He finishes with the bed.* MARGO *prepares to leave.*)

I be honest with you. Is been a long time since I been with a woman.

MARGO: (*Disinterested*) Oh yeah?

HECTOR: Like a year.

MARGO: That's too bad.

HECTOR: I was in the hospital.

(*Pause*)

MARGO: (*More interested*) The hospital?

HECTOR: Yeah.

MARGO: What was wrong with you?

HECTOR: Just resting up.

MARGO: You rest up at home, Mister. Not in the hospital.

HECTOR: Little case of nerves, you know?

MARGO: (*Not convinced*) Uh huh.

(*Pause*)

I really hope you're not BS-ing me here, chico. Because I can do real well without a case of something. You hear what I'm saying?

HECTOR: (*Approaching*) No, no. Nothin' like that. I tell you what is was ...

(MARGO, *putting her coat on, turns her back completely to* HECTOR.)

(*After a moment*) You interested in this?

MARGO: What?

HECTOR: I'm talking to you.

MARGO: (*Disinterested*) Yeah. Sure.

HECTOR: Would you believe the Dallas Cowboys put me in the hospital?

(*No response from* MARGO, *who gets her bag.*)

Is true. (*Short pause*) See, I used to make little bets on things.

(*As* HECTOR *speaks he will block the door by leaning on it. Not a menacing move on* HECTOR'S *part, simply one to keep her there a bit longer.*)

MARGO: Uh huh.

HECTOR: Horses, boxing, all that stuff. And see, pretty soon I started to make bigger and bigger bets. Bets so big my wife say, "Goodbye Hector."

MARGO: Right.

HECTOR: Hey. I had some pretty good opportunities. Pretty good mechanic's job for awhile.

MARGO: I got to go.

HECTOR: Nothing matters to me. All I want is one big hit.

MARGO: Right. Look. I gotta go.

HECTOR: So. Cowboys playin' the Colts. Bookie says to me, "I give you the Colts with eight." (*Beat*) Hey, the Colts a good team! You kidding me?! (*Beat*) And I take everything. I beg, I borrow ... Everything.

MARGO: Come on. I'm not playing here. All right?

HECTOR: Dallas Cowboys 16, Baltimore Colts 3. (*Beat*) You know how many times I added 8 and 3? Tried to come up with 17? (*He approaches*) I don't remember so good after that. Some crazy doctor say I run into the street and stab myself a buncha times with a kitchen knife. (*He opens his shirt.*)

MARGO: Get away from me.

HECTOR: Maybe I did. I mean. I got the cuts.

MARGO: Get the fuck away from me!

HECTOR: What are you talking about?

MARGO: You think I don't know your type?

HECTOR: Hey, I'm just trying to talk to you.

MARGO: I know your type. Mr. Kitchen Knife. Mr. Sicko.

(*She opens the door.* EMIL, *with his key out, stares at her.*)

I didn't just get off a bus from Utica!

(MARGO *steals a quick look at* EMIL *as she brushes past.* EMIL *stares after her a moment before entering.*)

HECTOR: (*Calls*) You miss the point! The point is now I gamble on Hector Diaz and that's all I gamble on!

EMIL: Hector?

(*No response.*)

Who was that?

HECTOR: (*Adjusting his shirt*) Nobody. Some crazy woman.

EMIL: (*Closing the door*) What did she want?

HECTOR: Is not important.

EMIL: Where were you?

HECTOR: Me?

(EMIL *is taking off his coat and draping it over the chair. One side of his face is red and he tries to keep that side turned from* HECTOR.)

EMIL: I ran down the hall as soon as the landlady told me you were on the phone. I did exactly like you said. I walked outside, I turned by the newspaper stand, I walked three blocks and I waited by the bus stop. (*Short pause*) Waited five buses, Hector.

HECTOR: Yeah, well see I tried to call back and tell you not to bother but I was too late. You were gone.

EMIL: Who was that woman?

HECTOR: Never mind that woman, Emil.

EMIL: So what did you want me for?

HECTOR: (*Smiles*) Because I couldn't wait to tell you. I got good news. I got a job. (*He takes a business card from his shirt pocket, hands it to* EMIL.)

EMIL: What's it say?

HECTOR: (*Indicating the words on the card.*) "Arturo's Auto Center." (*Short pause*) I start tomorrow. (*He returns the card to his pocket. Pause.*)

EMIL: (*Unhappy*) That's good, Hector.

HECTOR: Ain't that good?

(EMIL *nods*)

Hey, I was almost ready to give up after yesterday. Now today. First place I go—bang.

EMIL: Good. (EMIL *goes to the left chair, sits. Pause.*)

HECTOR: (*Approaching*) Hey, what's the matter with you?

EMIL: Nothing.

HECTOR: What.

EMIL: Nothing.

(*Pause*)

HECTOR: Hey, I know what's the matter. You afraid once I get the money coming in, I'm gonna forget about you. Take off and leave you someplace. Is that what you think? (EMIL *shrugs*. HECTOR *sits on the bed and faces him.*) Emil, I swear to you before

Jesus, we will stick together. As long as you do what I ask you to do we will be like this. (*He holds up his index and middle fingers pressed tightly together. He rises.*) AND WE WILL RISE TO THE TOP AS A TEAM! (*Pause*) Okay, man?

EMIL: (*After a moment, smiles.*) 'Kay.

(*Pause.* HECTOR *notices* EMIL'S *face.*)

HECTOR: Hey, Emil, what happened to your face?

(*No response*)

Is all red.

(EMIL *shrugs*)

You fall or somethin'?

EMIL: No.

HECTOR: Somebody punch you or something?

EMIL: (*Hesitates*) No.

HECTOR: What? Tell me.

EMIL: (*After a moment*) Well this morning while you were out I wanted to play the saxophone a little.

HECTOR: Yeah ...

EMIL: And I was doing "Take the 'A' Train" and there was a knock on the door and it was the landlady's son from downstairs.

HECTOR: The great big guy?

EMIL: The great big guy. And he told me to cut out the noise so I told him what you said. That this is my house and I can do anything I want.

HECTOR: He hit you, man?

EMIL: He picked me up by my face.

HECTOR: The son-of-a-bitch!

EMIL: I really like being your roommate, Hector, and I like handling the money and everything, but I want to be able to play the saxophone without somebody picking me up by the face.

HECTOR: The great big guy.

(EMIL *nods*.)

Emil, listen to me. I'm gonna have us out of here as soon as I get some money. I promise you. (*Short pause*) But maybe until then you should just cool it.

EMIL: Not play you mean.

HECTOR: Just for a little while.

EMIL: I got to play, Hector.

HECTOR: Just for a couple of weeks.

EMIL: I got to play!

HECTOR: Then play outside! In the park or somethin'!

EMIL: I wouldn't've come if I knew I couldn't play!

HECTOR: I don't make the fuckin' rules, Emil!

(*Pause*)

EMIL: You promised.

HECTOR: I'm sorry, okay?

(*Pause*)

EMIL: Not your fault. You don't make the fuckin' rules.

(*Pause.* HECTOR *goes to the mirror, fixes his hair with a pocket comb. After a moment* EMIL *rises, approaches*.)

EMIL: I was thinking.

HECTOR: Hey. Is that what I smell burning?

(HECTOR *laughs at this.* EMIL *smiles*.)

EMIL: We could save a lot of money if we got a cheaper place.

HECTOR: No, no. We find any place, we find a better place.

EMIL: I wouldn't mind a cheaper place, Hector. I really wouldn't. (*Short pause*) Maybe in a cheaper place they wouldn't care if I played the saxophone.

(HECTOR *puts the comb away.*)

HECTOR: Emil. I'm gonna get us a place so nice that when you play that saxophone, people in tuxedos will cheer from the other rooms.

EMIL: You promise?

HECTOR: You can count on it.

(*Pause*)

EMIL: Hey, Hector. Let's celebrate.

HECTOR: For what?

EMIL: Your job!

HECTOR: Hey, is no big thing.

EMIL: A nice dinner!

HECTOR: Is not necessary, man.

EMIL: We'll get your favorite. What's your favorite? What do you like?

(HECTOR *shrugs as he watches* EMIL *open the case and rummage through. After a moment,* EMIL *stops.*)

HECTOR: What's wrong, man?

(EMIL *takes a few bills from the case.*)

EMIL: We only got $7.

HECTOR: No. (*Approaches*) You sure?

EMIL: We had $32 before I left here!

HECTOR: Maybe you counted wrong.

EMIL: I don't make mistakes with money, Hector!

HECTOR: Okay, well lemme look. (*He quickly looks through the case.*) Shit. (*He closes the case.*) I hate to tell you this, Emil, but we been ripped off, man. We should never leave money in the room like this. Is my fault. I take total blame, man. (*He puts the case on the floor.*) You know what we gotta do. We gotta stretch that seven till next week. Till I get my first pay check. That's what we gotta do. (*He lies back on the bed. Long pause.*)

EMIL: You're lying to me.

HECTOR: What?

EMIL: You think I'm stupid.

HECTOR: (*Sitting up*) You watch who you call a liar, Emil.

EMIL: I knew I should've taken it with me! I knew it!

HECTOR: (*Gets up, approaches*) Call the wrong person a liar get you punched right in your mouth.

EMIL: You told me on the phone! Leave it! Somebody might try and grab it away!

HECTOR: I'm trying to look out for you, man!

EMIL: You lied to me!

HECTOR: You better watch it, Emil!

(*Banging on the wall from an adjacent room.*)

EMIL: You promised you'd never lie to me!

HECTOR: You nuts, man, you know that?!

EMIL: Who would rob us and leave $7?!

HECTOR: Hey, don't ask me! I ain't God!

(*More forceful banging on the wall. A VOICE yells: KEEP IT THE FUCK DOWN IN THERE!!*)

EMIL: And plus leave a saxophone that's worth about a million bucks!

(*The banging continues*)

HECTOR: They're nuts down here, Emil! (*He indicates the wall.*) You hear that?! They're crazy! They do stuff like that! (*Short pause, then toward the wall:*) SHUT UP MOTHER-FUCKER BEFORE I COME IN THERE AND KILL YOU!

(*One final thud on the wall, which knocks plaster to the floor.*)

(*To himself*) Crazy motherfucker. (*He goes to the window, stares out.*)

EMIL: You gave that woman $25.

HECTOR: Hey, if that's what you want to believe, I can't stop you.

EMIL: You waited until I wasn't around and you snuck it.

(HECTOR *turns from the window, faces* EMIL.)

HECTOR: You can really bring down a celebration, you know that? You can really throw cold water on a good time.

EMIL: Go find that woman and get our $25 back.

HECTOR: C'mon, man. I can't do that.

EMIL: YOU DO IT!

(*Long pause*)

HECTOR: Emil, I want you to sit down over here.

(EMIL *hesitates*)

C'mere.

(EMIL *approaches, sits, hugs the saxophone case.*)

Now after I say what I have to say, if you still want to call me a liar, you can put on your coat and get out. There's no point in us being roommates if we can't trust each other.

(*Pause*)

Okay.

(*Pause*)

I'm walking down Tenth Avenue today feeling very, very sad. (*He walks toward the window, stops, looks out.*) I'm asking myself. How can you let poor Emil down the way you keep doing, man? How can you do that to him?

EMIL: I just think——

HECTOR: Quiet, Emil. Lemme finish.

(*Pause*)

And finally it gets to me, man. I fall on my knees. On Tenth Avenue. Emil. On the cold sidewalk. I fall to my knees and I pray to the Virgin Mary to please, *please* help me! (*Beat*) To help us. (*Short pause*) And I make a promise, Emil, that if the Virgin, in her wonderful and divine mercy, will help us, I will give a part of my first day's pay—in advance—to the first needy soul who passes my way.

(*Pause*)

Then I hear a voice, Emil. Like a miracle. While I'm still on my knees on Tenth Avenue. The voice of Arturo himself! And I get up and I go inside and I get a job. A job, Emil!

(*Pause*)

Hey, well, I keep my promises, man. And as soon as I leave Arturo's and I see that poor fallen woman, I know.

(*Pause*)

And that, Emil, is where our $25 went. To pay my debt to the holy mother of God.

(*Pause*)

Now. If you still want to call me a liar, you should do what I say. Put on your coat and get out.

(*Pause. EMIL hesitates, gets his coat, exits carrying saxophone in case. He closes the door after he exits. Long pause. HECTOR suddenly rushes to the door, opens it, calls*:)

HECTOR: HEY, WELL FUCK YOU, MAN! I DON'T NEED YOU! YOU DON'T EVEN LISTEN! WHO THE FUCK NEEDS YOU WHEN YOU DON'T EVEN LISTEN?!

BLACKOUT
Scene Three

(TIME: *Early evening, the following day.* HECTOR *stares out the window. His jacket is across the back of the right center chair. After a moment there is a knock on the door.*)

HECTOR: (*Turns toward the door.*) Emil?

(*Short pause.* HECTOR *goes to the door, unlocks and opens it.* MRS. FIRESTONE, *the landlady, stands in the doorway. She wears a sweater over a shapeless housedress.*)

MRS. FIRESTONE: You told my boy you wanted something?

HECTOR: Would you come in, please?

(*With suspicion, she enters.*)

MRS. FIRESTONE: Sixty-eight degrees. Right up to code. Bring in a thermometer.

HECTOR: Is no problem.

MRS. FIRESTONE: Exterminator comes every other Monday.

HECTOR: Is about this. (HECTOR *takes out a half-sheet of paper from his shirt, unfolds it.*)

MRS. FIRESTONE: What about it?

HECTOR: Was scotch-taped over the mailboxes.

MRS. FIRESTONE: (*Lightly snatching the paper.*) Where it's supposed to be.

HECTOR: I want the job.

(*Pause*)

MRS. FIRESTONE: You do, huh?

(HECTOR *nods*)

MRS. FIRESTONE: You got qualifications?

HECTOR: I can swing a mop. Change a lightbulb.

MRS. FIRESTONE: How do you put in a dimmer switch?

HECTOR: Well ... you take out the old switch and put in the dimmer switch.

MRS. FIRESTONE: (*Short pause*) Right. I'll keep you in mind.

(MRS. FIRESTONE *turns to go.* HECTOR *grabs her arm.*)

HECTOR: Listen, Miss——

MRS. FIRESTONE: Firestone. And it's "Mrs." (*Looks at his hand.*) And keep your hands to yourself.

HECTOR: (*Withdraws his hand*) I really don't need no big wage or nothin'. All I need is maybe a room.

(*Pause.* MRS. FIRESTONE *is listening.*)

See, 'cause I got money. I get this government pension so
there's plenty of money, but I need a little something to keep
me busy, you know?

(*No response.*)

Totally on the up-and-up, here. I swear to you.

MRS. FIRESTONE: I don't need more headaches from the
Immigration people.

HECTOR: No headaches.

MRS. FIRESTONE: I don't need people banging on my door
at two in the morning.

HECTOR: No, no.

(MRS. FIRESTONE *checks him out.*)

MRS. FIRESTONE: So I'm going to walk into the furnace
room some morning, find you reading *Playboy* with your
draws down?

HECTOR: No way. I promise you. Like money in the bank.
Never late, never sick, never a bad word.

MRS. FIRESTONE: Money in the bank, huh?

HECTOR: Just like money from home.

(*Pause*)

MRS. FIRESTONE: Well, even if I did, I couldn't give you
this room. This is one of my best rooms. I could rent this
room to people with luggage. We're dealing with a view over
here.

(*Pause*)

I do have this room in the basement. (*Short pause*) Lousy City
won't let me rent—fire codes or some crap ... (*Short pause*)
Basically the same set-up as this. Cement floor, no window,
but basically the same set-up.

HECTOR: Sounds okay to me.

MRS. FIRESTONE: I suppose I could stick a folding bed in there. Call it a workshop. (*Beat*) When's your week up here?

HECTOR: Three days.

(MRS. FIRESTONE *nods, starts for the door.*)

So I got it?

MRS. FIRESTONE: Give it a shot.

HECTOR: Hey, well thank you, Mrs. Firestone. I promise you. I'll have this place looking like a diamond.

MRS. FIRESTONE: Yeah. (*She has moved to the door, stops, faces* HECTOR.) What happened to the ... What was he? A retard?

HECTOR: His name is Emil.

MRS. FIRESTONE: You didn't kill him, did you?

HECTOR: I think he went home. Pennsylvania somewhere.

MRS. FIRESTONE: Just so long as you didn't kill him. (*Short pause*) I put up with a lot of nonsense here, but I have to draw a line. You know?

(HECTOR *nods*)

What's your name?

HECTOR: Diaz. Hector.

MRS. FIRESTONE: All right. Diaz Hector. 8 o'clock Monday morning. We'll see what you can do.

HECTOR: Hey, well you won't be sorry.

MRS. FIRESTONE: And look. If I do happen to walk in the furnace room one morning and catch you with your pants down ... (*Short pause, smiles*) We'll handle it. (*She stares at* HECTOR *another moment, exits, closes door. Pause.*)

HECTOR: (*To himself*) Oh, yeah? That's what you think. (*Mock laugh. He goes to the window, gazes out.*) A view. (*Mock laugh. He goes to the bed, sits on it with his feet up and his back propped by the pillows. After a moment he reaches toward his jacket and* withdraws the business card. He studies it a moment, reads:) "Arturo's Auto Center." (*Short pause*) Good-bye. (*He pinches the card, sends it across the room. Pause. He lies back on the bed and stares at the ceiling. The door slowly opens.* EMIL, *carrying the saxophone case, looks into the room.*)

EMIL: Hector?

HECTOR: (*Sitting up*) Emil.

EMIL: I thought you'd be at work.

(HECTOR *sits on the side of the bed, faces* EMIL.)

HECTOR: No, no. I'm home. (*Pause*) So come on in.

(EMIL *does*)

Close the door.

(EMIL *closes the door.*)

Sit.

(EMIL *sits in stage left chair.*)

EMIL: (*After a moment*) How come you're not at work?

HECTOR: (*Laughs*) Would you believe if I told you I got fired already?

EMIL: How come?

HECTOR: (*To himself*) How come. (*He rises, paces*) I get to work nice and early. I'm ready to go, this guy—this punk, Arturo's son or something—starts telling me what to do! (*Beat*) "Drop the oil in that Mercury! Get that pick-up on a lift! Hand me the air-gun! Do this! Do that! (*Short pause*) Not even a fuckin' cup of coffee, man. (*Pause*) So I go along as much as I can but finally, I can't do it no more. (*Short pause, calls:*) You want somebody to drop the oil in that Mercury?! You drop it! You need some help, come and get me! I'll help you drop it! I'll drop it right on your fuckin' face!

EMIL: That's when you got fired?

(*Pause*)

HECTOR: No.

EMIL: No?

(HECTOR *moves to the window but keeps his eyes on* EMIL.)

HECTOR: Hey, the truth is, I got there and Arturo wouldn't hire me. (*Pause*) Is not all my fault, Emil. They got computers, they got whatchacall ... dynometers, they got all this new electronic shit ...!

(*Pause.* HECTOR *approaches.*)

HECTOR: What can I say? No big deal. Already I got something else.

EMIL: You do?

HECTOR: No big money or nothing. Free room. That's something. (*Pause*) See, I worked out a deal with the landlady. I look after the building, she gives me a free room. (*Short pause*) Not this room. I told her I don't want no room five flights up. Want a nice room downstairs. (*Short pause*) Hey, I figure I get a night job, take care of the building during the day ... Piece of cake.

(*Long pause*)

EMIL: I'm sorry I called you a liar.

HECTOR: Hey, well you hurt me, man.

EMIL: I'm sorry.

HECTOR: You got to learn. Sometimes being sorry ain't enough.

(*Pause*)

EMIL: I love you, Hector.

HECTOR: Hey, c'mon, Emil. (*Approaches*) Somebody hears you ... you know, could be embarrassing, man. (*Pause*) Gimme your coat.

(EMIL *stands, takes off his coat, hands it to* HECTOR *who walks to the chair and hangs it over the back.*)

So where'd you sleep?

EMIL: Didn't.

HECTOR: You been up all night?

EMIL: Uh huh.

HECTOR: You see? You learn something. I don't take care of you, nobody gonna take care of you.

EMIL: (*Smiles*) It was the best night of my life. (*Pause*) Not that it started out so great. I was walking so much my feet were killing me. So I stood by this store and watched the people and then it started getting dark and I remembered what you said. (*Beat*) That if I wanted to play I should go outside. (*Short pause*) So that's what I did. (*Short pause*) And some people started to listen, Hector. They listened so hard I was scared to stop. Somebody yelled for me to open my case and I was scared not to.

HECTOR: Emil, you gotta be careful out there, baby.

EMIL: Some people dropped money in.

(*Pause*)

HECTOR: You kidding.

EMIL: I played for a couple of hours. Then this man came over. He told me he didn't want to disturb me when I was playing, but what was I doing on his corner.

HECTOR: (*Sensing a scam*) His corner.

EMIL: That's what he said. He said he usually don't let nobody play on his corner but he liked "my sound." (EMIL, *pleased with this, laughs*.) He said if I give him some money, I can play there anytime I want. He'll protect me.

HECTOR: Protect you from what?

EMIL: He didn't say.

HECTOR: I hope you didn't give him nothing, Emil.

EMIL: He took $15.

HECTOR: You made $15?

EMIL: I made $43 and 27¢.

(*Pause*)

HECTOR: You shitting me.

EMIL: Uh uh. (EMIL *goes to the bed, opens the saxophone case. He lifts the instrument. Sees cash, primarily change.*) See?

(HECTOR *stares at the money.*)

That's why I came back. I thought you'd be at work. I was gonna leave you some money so you wouldn't be mad at me anymore.

HECTOR: *You* were gonna leave *me* some money.

EMIL: And the key. I forgot to leave my key.

(*Pause*)

HECTOR: Emil, I don't want you out there like that no more, man. Is dangerous.

EMIL: Silky says——

HECTOR: Who?

EMIL: The man who runs the corner. (*Pause*) Silky says I don't have to worry. He'll take care of things.

HECTOR: Oh, yeah? Well lemme tell you something about "Silky." "Silky" could be anything. He could be a cop, he could be a junkie, he could be a … anything.

EMIL: But he lets me play.

HECTOR: Is not the most important thing!

EMIL: To me it is.

(*Pause*)

HECTOR: You want to wind up dead?

EMIL: No.

HECTOR: Well that's what's gonna happen, you don't listen to me. (*Long pause*) Okay. Sit down. Lemme explain to you.

(EMIL *sits on the edge of the bed.* HECTOR *sits next to him.*)

Two people live together.

EMIL: Like you and me.

HECTOR: Could be like you and me. Could be like a mother and father. (*Pause*) Now with these two people, one gotta lead and one gotta watch. Right?

EMIL: I guess so.

HECTOR: The father—the man—he leads. He works, he brings in money, he takes care of things ... The mother watches this. She tells him how he's doing. That except for him, she could not live. Very important. (*Pause*) Now you could never have two fathers living together. Or two mothers living together. Too much leading on one side, too much watching on the other. (*Pause*) Is the same with us. (*Indicates himself*) One leader (*Indicates* EMIL), one watcher.

EMIL: You don't want me to play the saxophone no more.

HECTOR: Is not the point, Emil! The point is, I don't want you out in the street where you could be killed for few lousy bucks! Not when I have the training and ability to bring in $25 an hour! (*Pause*) You wanna play the saxophone, play it for me. (*Short pause*) Just don't play it here or we both be on the sidewalk. (*Pause*) And be patient! (*Short pause*) I got us someplace to live today. That's something.

EMIL: (*After a moment, to himself.*) It's not enough.

(*Pause*)

HECTOR: You say something?

EMIL: (*Short pause, then directly to* HECTOR.) It's not enough.

BLACKOUT
Scene Four

(TIME: *Two days later, close to midnight. The room is in near-total darkness.* EMIL *enters from the hall. He now wears a brightly colored scarf around his neck. He closes the door and fumbles in the dark.*)

HECTOR: (*Dark*) Turn it on.

EMIL: (*Dark*) Hector?

HECTOR: (*Dark*) Turn it on.

(EMIL, *at the wall switch, turns on the lamp. He is carrying his saxophone case.* HECTOR, *barefooted, is seated in the chair and turned three-quarters looking out the window. His socks are hanging over the lampshade.* EMIL *carries two paper bags: one from Dunkin Donuts and the other from Woolworth.*)

EMIL: I was trying to be quiet. I thought you'd be asleep.

HECTOR: Do I look asleep?

(*No response. Pause.*)

I like to sit in the dark and look out, okay?

EMIL: For two days?

HECTOR: Yeah, for two days. What are you? A fuckin' cop?

(EMIL *moves toward the bed; after a moment.*)

What the hell's on your neck?

EMIL: (*Approaching, taking the scarf off.*) Silky gave it to me.

HECTOR: Silky ...

EMIL: It's warm. Try it.

HECTOR: Get the fuckin' thing away from me.

(EMIL *puts the scarf on the bed.*)

EMIL: I wanted to drop these off. Silky's waiting for me in the coffee shop across the street.

HECTOR: Well we don't want to keep Silky waiting, do we?

EMIL: I just saw the landlady on the steps. I asked her if I could see the new room. (*Pause*) It's in the cellar, Hector. (*Pause*) I gave her ten bucks to hold this room for another week.

HECTOR: You did what?!

EMIL: I gave her ten bucks to——

HECTOR: I set that up!

EMIL: I figured we'd be better up here.

HECTOR: You figured. (*Beat*) Well you stay up here. You don't tell me what to do. (*Pause*)

EMIL: I got some Dunkin Donuts.

HECTOR: If I wanted Dunkin Donuts, I'd get my own Dunkin Donuts.

(EMIL *opens the Woolworth bag, takes out a cheap transistor radio, turns it on, sets it on top of the dresser. A jazz station, with less than perfect reception, plays.* EMIL *smiles, looks over at* HECTOR *for approval. No response from* HECTOR.)

The man in the store showed me how it works. (*Short pause*) You can listen to it anytime you want.

(EMIL *goes back to the Woolworth bag.*)

And I got something else. Two for nine dollars. One for me, one for you.

(EMIL *takes out two different-colored flannel shirts.*)

Flannel. Very warm.

(*Pause.* HECTOR *reaches out, takes one of the shirts, studies it, tosses it on the bed.*)

HECTOR: I can't wear this.

EMIL: Wrong size?

HECTOR: Is a cowboy shirt! I look like a cowboy?!

EMIL: Lotta people wear these shirts. You don't have to be a cowboy.

HECTOR: I hate the shirt, Emil, okay?! What can I say?! You my mother now?! You pick out my clothes?!

(*Pause.* EMIL *rises, goes toward the dresser with both shirts.*)

EMIL: I'll put them away.

HECTOR: You do that.

(EMIL *puts one shirt in top drawer, one in drawer underneath.*)

(*Sarcastically*) You "play" tonight?

(EMIL *ignores the sarcasm, faces* HECTOR, *smiles.*)

EMIL: Almost nine hours. (*He goes to the bed, picks up the sax-ophone case.*) I had over $90 in here when I got done. Made a hundred-and-thirty-something. Silky took $45, I got the rest. (*He sits on the bed with the saxophone case on his lap. He opens it, takes out some bills, counts them.*)

HECTOR: (*After a moment*) Well I hope you enjoy it, I really do. (*Pause*) Because it's all gonna come down around your ears very soon, Emil. People get very tired of the same old saxo-phone music. Couple days, you can't make a fuckin' dime.

(EMIL *has taken out a few bills. He extends them toward* HECTOR.)

EMIL: Here.

HECTOR: What.

EMIL: Money.

HECTOR: I know it's money. I've seen money.

(*Pause.* EMIL *puts the cash back in the saxophone case, leaves the case open on the bed.*)

EMIL: Eat today?

HECTOR: None of your business.

EMIL: Doughnut?

HECTOR: No!

(*Pause*)

EMIL: Just trying to help.

HECTOR: You wanna help, leave me alone.

EMIL: You always helped me. (*Pause*) We always shared the money when we got out of the crazy house.

HECTOR: Was different.

EMIL: How come?

HECTOR: Because it was mine! I came up with the plan! I got you to take the money! You wouldn't've listened to nobody else! (*Pause*) I worked for that money, Emil! I didn't do nothing to get (*Indicates* EMIL'S *money*) this shit! (*Pause. He stares out the window.*) (*Mock laugh*) Look at me. Hector Diaz. No job. No dignity. (*Beat*) One pair of socks every morning still wet from the night before ...

(*Long pause*)

EMIL: You need some new socks?

(*Pause.* HECTOR *rises, approaches* EMIL.)

HECTOR: Lemme explain something to you. (*Pause*) You take something from somebody, you know what that means? (*Beat*) Means you his. (*Short pause*) Is okay if it's your boss or your wife or something, that's okay. (*Short pause*) But for *me* to take from *you* ... (*He stares at* EMIL. *Pause. He returns to the chair, looks out.*)

EMIL: (*After a moment*) I could give you a job.

(*Pause.* HECTOR *faces* EMIL.)

HECTOR: (*Mock laugh*) What?

EMIL: Partners. We split fifty/fifty.

HECTOR: I work for you?

EMIL: You could keep the people back. (*Short pause*) Sometimes the coins land on the sidewalk and other people pick them up.

HECTOR: You would want me to pick them up.

EMIL: We split fifty/fifty.

HECTOR: (*Rises*) I could dress up like a monkey ... (*He mimics an organ grinder's monkey.*) ... dance around while you play.

EMIL: (*Short pause*) We could try it.

(*Pause*)

HECTOR: Okay, Emil. You want to give me something? Lemme give you something. Lesson in life. (*He opens the window. Some night noise—a typical Saturday night at midnight.*) I want you to watch very close. (*He moves to the bed, quickly snatches the saxophone from the case.*)

EMIL: Hey!

(HECTOR *quickly moves to the window holding the saxophone. He holds the instrument, by the mouthpiece, out the window.* EMIL *quickly rushes over.*)

HECTOR: Any closer and I let it go, Emil. I'm not kiddin'.

(EMIL *freezes*)

You see? This is the difference between you and me. I let go of this and it's over for you, man. No more saxophone, no more Emil. (*Pause*) Hey, well sure, you could buy a new one, but it wouldn't change nothing. Somebody could still take it away from you easy. Bang. Out the window. (*Pause*) But I have ability, Emil. A brain. I can think. Nobody can take that away. (*Pause*) You want your saxophone?

EMIL: (*Still frozen*) Gimme my saxophone.

HECTOR: Please?

(*Pause*)

EMIL: Please.

(*Pause.* HECTOR *brings the instrument back inside, extends it toward* EMIL. EMIL *hesitates a moment before clutching the saxophone. Without putting the instrument back in the case, he closes the case, pick it up, starts for the door.*)

EMIL: (*Stops*) Don't you ever do that again, Hector.

HECTOR: So what if I do? What are gonna do? Kill me?

EMIL: (*At the door, facing* HECTOR) No. (*Pause*) But I won't come back, either.

(EMIL *exits.* HECTOR *stares at the closed door for a moment.*)

HECTOR: (*To himself*) So don't.

(*Pause.* HECTOR *shivers, rubs his arms. He looks toward the open window, approaches it, attempts to pull it shut. It's stuck. He curses, bangs on the window, gives up. Pause. He goes to the dresser and roughly turns off the transistor. He starts back, sees the doughnut bag, stops. He picks it up. He sits, stares out the open window, takes a doughnut from the bag, takes a bite. He stops. Pause. A moment of realization. He sticks what's left of the doughnut back in the bag, throws the bag across the room, wipes his mouth. He sits back. Pause. He rises, slowly climbs out on the window ledge. After a moment or two, reenter* EMIL. EMIL *quickly snatches the scarf he'd left on the bed, starts for the door. He stops, studies the room, looks toward the window.*)

EMIL: Hector? (EMIL *puts his saxophone case on the bed and cautiously approaches the window.*)

HECTOR: (*Outside*) Get away from me, Emil!

(EMIL *stops by the window.*)

I'm serious! I'm not kidding with you! (*Short pause*) GET OUTTA HERE, MAN!

EMIL: It's all right, Hector.

HECTOR: (*Outside*) Get outta here, man.

EMIL: Give me your hand.

HECTOR: (*Outside*) (*Frozen*) I don't need you.

EMIL: Come on.

(*Long pause*)

HECTOR: (*Outside*) (*Nervous laugh*) I can't move.

EMIL: It's okay, Hector.

HECTOR: (*Outside*) (*Nervous, almost frantic laugh.*) I can't fuckin' move.

EMIL: Hector?

HECTOR: (*Outside*) Help me, Emil.

EMIL: Come on.

HECTOR: (*Outside*) Help me.

EMIL: Give me your hand.

(HECTOR *does*)

Swing your leg in.

(HECTOR *does*)

Watch your head. Watch your head!

(*After a moment,* HECTOR *is inside.* EMIL, *with an arm around him, supports* HECTOR'S *weight. They pause together.*)

HECTOR: (*With relief*) Whuu. (*Pause*) (*Slight laugh*) Some scary shit out there, man.

EMIL: It's okay.

HECTOR: (*Laughs*) Little tiny people and cars and shit.

(EMIL *has led him to the edge of the bed. Both sit.* EMIL'S *arm still supporting* HECTOR.)

EMIL: You all right?

HECTOR: Yeah. Sure. (*Pause*) Whuu. (*He laughs. Pause.*) So listen. I was thinking. Maybe the weekends, I got nothing to do. I could help you out. "Strong-arm" for you. You know, keep an eye on things while you busy playing.

EMIL: All right.

HECTOR: Is not a bad room downstairs, man. Just takes a little getting used to, right?

EMIL: Right.

(*Pause*)

HECTOR: Thanks, Emil.

EMIL: It's okay.

HECTOR: Thanks.

EMIL: It's okay.

(*Pause.* EMIL *goes to the window, closes it.* HECTOR *stands.* *Pause.*)

HECTOR: You wanna know something else?

(EMIL *looks toward* HECTOR.)

The fuckin' doughnuts were stale.

BLACKOUT

CURTAIN

Property List

ONSTAGE

Double bed with frayed bedspread and two pillows, center
Straight-backed chair, right center
Straight-backed chair, left center
Standing lamp with lampshade, upper right center
Wooden dresser with mirror, down right center
Debris on dresser: coffee cups, empty bag from diner, napkins. (Strike after Scene One.)
Rug, down right center

SCENE ONE

Saxophone (EMIL)
Saxophone case (EMIL)
Emil's ski jacket (Across back of left center chair)
Stage money in saxophone case—$37 and loose change (Includes one five-dollar bill and three singles.)
Cigarettes (HECTOR)

SCENE TWO

Coat (MARGO) across left center chair
Handbag (MARGO) on left center chair
Coat (HECTOR) across right center chair
Lipstick (MARGO)
Business card—"Arturo's Auto Center," (HECTOR)
Pocket comb (HECTOR)
Stage money in saxophone case—$7 and loose change

SCENE THREE

Half-sheet of paper with handwritten janitor's job offer. (HECTOR)
Stage money in saxophone case—approximately $50 in bills and change
Room key (EMIL)

SCENE FOUR

Scarf (EMIL)
Socks (HECTOR'S) draped over lampshade
Paper bag (Dunkin Donuts) containing doughnuts (EMIL)
Second paper bag (Woolworth's) containing:
     Transistor radio
     One flannel shirt (HECTOR'S size)
     One flannel shirt (EMIL'S size)
Stage money—approximately $90 in bills and change

Costume Plot

HECTOR
   Brown leather jacket
   Black pants
   Faded acrylic shirt
   White leather shoes
   Black socks
   Brown felt hat

EMIL
   Ski jacket—brightly colored and dirty
   Polyester pants
   Plaid cotton shirt
   Suede shoes
   Brightly colored scarf (Scene Four)

MARGO
   Imitation fur coat
   Vinyl "leather-look" skirt
   Low-cut black sweater
   Inexpensive boots
   Net stockings
   Beaded bag

MRS. FIRESTONE
   Flowered housedress
   Man's green sweater
   White socks
   Slippers

KATHARINE LONG

KATHARINE LONG graduated from Kenyon College in 1977, the same year her play *The Attic* was chosen as a finalist in the Actor's Theatre of Louisville Great American Play Contest. She became a member of the Ensemble Studio Theatre in 1978. Since then, several of her plays have been produced there including *Unseen Friends* in Marathon '79 and *Two-Part Harmony* in Marathon '80. *Two-Part Harmony* was produced again in E.S.T.'s *Three from the Marathon* in 1981.

Although a resident of New York City, Ms. Long's work reflects her Mid-west origins. *Unseen Friends* takes place in Oak Grove, Missouri, circa 1932, where her father was raised. *Ariel Bright* is set in Grayson, Missouri, circa 1912, a town so small her mother had the distinction of being its only child. The setting for *Two-Part Harmony* is Champaign, Illinois, circa 1959, where Ms. Long herself was born.

As an actress, Ms. Long has performed the title role of *Ariel Bright* and has appeared in both the New York and Pittsburgh Public Theater productions of Arthur Giron's *Becoming Memories*.

Ariel Bright was first presented at the Marathon 1984 Festival of One-Act Plays in May, and subsequently produced in The Best of Marathon '84 at the Pepsico Summerfare Center for the Arts at SUNY Purchase. Both productions featured the following cast under the direction of John Schwab:

HILEY BEDSAL: Bill Cwikowski
ARIEL BRIGHT: Melodie Somers

Cornelia Twitchell was the stage manager; Jane Musky did the scenery; Karl E. Haas the lighting design; Linda Vigdor the costumes; and Bruce Ellman, the sound.

For Stock and amateur production rights, contact: Broadway Play Publishing, 357 W. 20th Street, New York, New York 10011. For all other rights, contact: Mary Harden, Bret Adams Ltd., 448 West 44th Street, New York, NY 10036.

ARIEL BRIGHT

By Katharine Long

For

Ruthanna Long

CHARACTERS

HILEY BEDSAL: Mid- to late-thirties; medium height, slight build. Moves quickly—always busy—adds personal touches to everything he does. Rarely spends time among the living.

ARIEL BRIGHT: Thirty-five; six-foot-one, slender, graceful, ethereal. Dressed in white. Heads turn when she walks down the street. A gifted actress, ahead of her time.

(TIME: *5:00 a.m. on August 6, 1912.* LOCALE: *Grayson, Missouri: A small town located in the western part of the state.* PLACE: *The back room of* HILEY BEDSAL'S *funeral parlor.*)

(*The back room is where bodies are prepared for their final departure. A drawn curtain, hanging upstage left, leads to the funeral parlor. Caskets can be purchased there when a funeral is not in progress.*)

(*As the lights go down, the first few bars of* "What A Friend We Have In Jesus" *softly plays to a ragtime beat. As the lights come up,* HILEY BEDSAL *is standing before the "work coffin", holding a playing card up to the corpse. Most morticians prepare their clients on a table, but* HILEY *feels that a work coffin helps acclimate the body to his or her new permanent home. This work coffin can be anything from a pine box to a portable tin bath, but whatever the style, it must conceal the body within. Mrs. Moxem is within and her white hair is visible.*)

(HILEY *has designed the back room to meet his specific needs. To the left stands a tall shelf containing cosmetics and other items. On the desk (upper right) is a typewriter, a filing box, and a few additional objects that denote "organization." A tombstone is on display—so is a clothes dummy, wearing a festive red gown. The gown is something a madam in a cat house might wear, and that is where* HILEY *got it.*)

HILEY: (*Holding a card before Mrs. Moxem*) Choosing a card is one thing. Finding it (*Returning the card to the deck.*) after hiding it (*Dispersing the deck into the base of the coffin.*) ... now that's something else. The trick is concentration. ... (*Reaching into the coffin, he pulls up not only the card, but the entire deck which falls into the shape of a "card castle."*) ... which isn't a trick at all. (*He removes a loose card from the top of the castle and shows it to her.*) Your card, dear lady. Thank you. (*The cards slip back into the base of the coffin.* HILEY *gathers the deck together.*) Last one. Lights out. Oh, you may not be tired now, but you will be—and tomorrow's a big day.

(*A long arm appears from behind the curtain.* HILEY *stares in astonishment as the curtain parts. The arm belongs to a woman who is alive and well and lying in one of* HILEY'S *display caskets.*)

HILEY: Miss Sneed!

ARIEL: Good evening.

HILEY: Good morning.

ARIEL: Is it morning already? How long did I sleep?

HILEY: How long have you been there?

ARIEL: You weren't here when I arrived. What time is it now?

HILEY: Four minutes past five.

ARIEL: Oh, thank goodness. I thought it was after six.

HILEY: How did you get in?

ARIEL: The parlor door was open.

HILEY: I beg to differ. It was locked.

ARIEL: The parlor door was easy to open.

(*She starts to get up;* HILEY *helps her out.*)

I hope you don't mind that I let myself in.

HILEY: As a matter of fact, I do.

(*She notices the corpse.*)

ARIEL: Did someone die while I was napping? I crossed my fingers that no one would. Dead people give me the willies.

HILEY: Just what are you doing here?

ARIEL: I'm waiting for the train.

HILEY: This is not the depot.

ARIEL: I tried waiting at the depot, but I arrived too early—hours ahead of time. So, I decided to take a walk—stretch my legs. By the time I reached your display window, I just felt compelled to lie down. ... That is one comfortable coffin. Cushions must be made of silk.

HILEY: They are.

ARIEL: From the street it looked like silk, but I couldn't be sure until I climbed inside.

HILEY: As a rule, I don't permit that. If I let everyone test out the caskets, why the cushions would tear and the wood would get scratched. (*He takes a cloth and begins wiping the wood of the casket she'd been in.*)

ARIEL: I understand the dilemma and I won't do it again. I promise.

HILEY: (*Handing her his business card.*) Good. Then you're always welcome in the parlor, when it's open, during shop hours. Of course, I don't open until 9 a.m.

ARIEL: (*Politely returning the card.*) During the day I'd be wasting your time. I'm not shopping to buy. I don't really need one ... How much are you asking for this particular model?

HILEY: Three hundred dollars.

ARIEL: God heavens! Sarah Bernhardt has one just like it. I wonder if she paid that much. Of course she bought hers in France. Things might be less expensive there.

HILEY: I wouldn't know.

ARIEL: Neither would I. But I would assume Miss Bernhardt could afford almost anything. I read in a recent article that she runs an extravagant household. Wild animals, including a leopard, occupy her salon. Salon is the Parisian word for parlor.

HILEY: Where does she keep this coffin?

ARIEL: In her bedroom.

HILEY: What's it doing there?

ARIEL: That's where she sleeps.

HILEY: In a coffin?

ARIEL: A bed for Miss Bernhardt would be mundane.

HILEY: Why?

ARIEL: She's the greatest actress of our time.

HILEY: What does a coffin have to do with it?

ARIEL: I'm not sure ... perhaps it relaxes her. In preparing for a demanding role, an actress must find solace somewhere. What could be more peaceful than the bed of eternal rest?

(ARIEL *smiles;* HILEY *doesn't.*)

The article didn't say exactly why she slept in one, but she does what she pleases and I admire everything she does.

(HILEY *is not convinced.*)

I'm sorry I jimmied the lock. I'll never do it again. (*She shakes his hand.*) Good-bye Mr. Bedsal. (*She starts to leave.*)

HILEY: Hold on there!

(*She stops dead in her tracts.*)

Call me Hiley.

ARIEL: Good-bye Hiley. Good-bye. ... (*Tentatively approaching the work coffin and peering in.*) ... Mrs. Moxem? Is that Mrs. Moxem?

HILEY: Who did you think it was?

ARIEL: I just assumed it was ... I don't know, some old tart.

HILEY: Why?

ARIEL: (*Referring to the clothes dummy.*) The dress. Is that her burial gown?

HILEY: (*Smiling proudly*) Don't you like it?

ARIEL: (*Politely*) It's nice—it's festive. But what would Mrs. Moxem think?

HILEY: I picked it out with her in mind.

ARIEL: But is it appropriate?

HILEY: For what?

ARIEL: For death.

HILEY: Almost anything will do.

ARIEL: But for a funeral. Her friends will be shocked.

HILEY: Her friends won't be there. She outlived everyone she liked. Everyone's gone, except me. And I wanted to go home earlier than I did, but she kept offering these cheddar cheese things and the card game lasted until 2 a.m ...

ARIEL: You were at her house this evening?

HILEY: Of course.

ARIEL: Who else was there?

HILEY: Just me.

ARIEL: How did she die?

HILEY: Laughing—at something I said. I don't remember being funny, but I guess she thought I was.

ARIEL: Is that why you ...

HILEY: What?

(ARIEL *peeks at the body*.)

Checking for marks?

ARIEL: Why would I do that?

HILEY: You think I killed her.

ARIEL: What a thought. It never occurred to me until you said it just now.

HILEY: I said, I just happened to be with her when she died.

ARIEL: Have you notified the authorities?

HILEY: I know how to do my job. I do it very well as a matter of fact. Do you think I really like cheddar cheese puff balls? I just ate them to be polite. And she cheats at cards. I knew that before we started playing—but I let her win. Everyone deserves a final pleasure. (*He begins brushing Mrs. Moxem's hair.*) And if I hadn't been with her, she would have died alone.

ARIEL: This evening?

HILEY: Oh yes.

ARIEL: How did you know?

HILEY: That she'd die tonight? It's hard to say.

ARIEL: It does seem strange that you just happened to be in the vicinity. And this isn't the first time I've noticed the coincidence. I'm referring to the untimely demise of Mr. Hopper.

HILEY: Of course I was around when he keeled over. Everyone in town was. It's not hard to be nearby in Grayson.

ARIEL: But you never paid him a speck of attention until the week before he died—and all that week you were pruning his bushes and mowing his lawn ...

HILEY: It needed doing and he wasn't going to get it done.

ARIEL: And what about Miss Twitchell?

HILEY: What about Miss Twitchell?

ARIEL: I was sure you were courting her and then two weeks into the courtship ... need I say more?

HILEY: I wasn't courting Miss Twitchell.

ARIEL: You took her to the horse show and you bought her that beautiful hat.

HILEY: I wanted to give her a final pleasure.

ARIEL: How did you know she needed one!

HILEY: I am not the kiss of death.

ARIEL: Then who are you! ... Please don't take offense, but in my opinion there is something unusual about you.

(HILEY *seems confused*)

Surely I am not the first to notice your distinction.

(HILEY *nods*)

Haven't you ever been told, by a close personal acquaintance perhaps that ...

HILEY: I don't have a close personal acquaintance.

ARIEL: Oh.

HILEY: Most of my friendships are made in passing.

ARIEL: I see. Then let me be the first to say that you are remarkably different from anyone I've ever met.

HILEY: Thank you. You are too. Delightfully so.

ARIEL: Sometimes different is not delightful. Sometimes it's just just plain odd.

HILEY: Please don't think that I would ever use that word to describe you.

ARIEL: Hiley, I'm using that word to describe you.

HILEY: How strange that you would come to that conclusion, considering we've never been formally introduced.

ARIEL: We didn't have to be. I've been watching you for quite some time.

HILEY: (*Pleased*) You have? Why?

ARIEL: You know things.

HILEY: Pardon?

ARIEL: You know more than a person should. Actually, you're more than odd. You're ...

HILEY: Odd is breaking into a funeral showroom and mussing up the caskets!

ARIEL: I only slept in one.

HILEY: Just the idea of doing what you did—laying in a coffin before your time. That is more than odd. That is grotesque.

ARIEL: Sarah Bernhardt does it!

HILEY: In Paris, France. You are from Paris, Kentucky.

ARIEL: How did you know that?

HILEY: I have a card on you in my file.

(HILEY *motions to the desk.* ARIEL *picks up the file box.* HILEY *nods and she opens it. She skims through the cards.*)

ARIEL: Why, you have a card on everyone in town.

HILEY: Filed alphabetically.

ARIEL: Why?

HILEY: I like organization.

ARIEL: But cards ...

HILEY: Listing birthdates and other pertinent facts. Can't order a tombstone unless I know when a person was born.

ARIEL: For the inscription?

HILEY: Believe me, it comes in handy. Everyone deserves a marker, but not everyone remembers to order one.

ARIEL: (*Regarding the tombstone on display.*) Did you make this yourself?

HILEY: No ... I order my tombstones from a company in Kansas City.

ARIEL: (*Reading the inscription*) "Mary Louise Moxem. Born August 6th 1813. Died August 6th ...

HILEY: 1912. Ninety-nine years old today. I brought a cake to her party. Made that myself. But we had those cheese puff things instead.

ARIEL: The tombstone arrived with the inscription?

HILEY: Oh yes.

ARIEL: When?

HILEY: Last week.

ARIEL: Now see what I mean. That is down right uncanny!

HILEY: I don't think so. Mailed the requisition form in last March.

(ARIEL *returns to the desk and frantically begins looking through the file.*)

HILEY: Can I be of assistance?

ARIEL: I'm not in here. I don't exist.

HILEY: Of course you do.

ARIEL: Then where am I? Seevers, Sinclair, Sleeper, no Sneed ...

HILEY: Try looking under Bright. Ariel Bright. You do prefer that don't you to Enid Sneed?

ARIEL: (*Taken aback*) Ariel Bright is not my Christian name.

HILEY: It's your stage name.

ARIEL: That's a secret.

(*He finds the card and sets it on the lid of the box.*)

HILEY: Ariel Bright.

ARIEL: It lists my birthdate and where I was born but it doesn't say anything about ...

(HILEY *crosses to the shelf and picks up several cosmetic tins.*)

HILEY: When you're going to die? No, I don't list everything.

ARIEL: But you know.

(HILEY *smiles and returns to the work coffin.*)

ARIEL: If you know, tell me. It's soon isn't it? I knew it all along. I haven't been feeling or looking my best. My hands are always cold—even in August and occasionally I feel this twinge ...

HILEY: Slow down. No need to rush things. You're not going to die young.

ARIEL: It's too late to die young. I'm thrity-five.

HILEY: You'll live to be twice that and more.

ARIEL: (*Takes a deep breath.*) How much more?

HILEY: A lot more.

ARIEL: How do you know?

HILEY: I just do.

ARIEL: I have time?

HILEY: Yes.

ARIEL: To do what I want to do? (*Her hand caresses the curtain. She runs her fingers along the wood of the casket she'd been in.*)

HILEY: If you set your mind to it. Quit fussing with that. Ariel, come away from there.

ARIEL: (*Returning from behind the curtain.*)
    "Grave sir, hail! I come
    To answer thy best pleasure; be't to fly, to swim, to dive
        into the fire:
    To ride on the curl'd clouds; to thy strong bidding task ...
    (*She curtsies.*) Ariel and all her quality.''

HILEY: (*Applauding*) That was very good.

ARIEL: Do you really think so?

HILEY: Oh yes.

ARIEL: I've never been on stage, but I've memorized every line from every play Shakespeare's ever written.

HILEY: And you say those lines with distinction.

ARIEL: Have you seen many plays?

HILEY: No. But I admire the theatre profession.

ARIEL: So do I. More than I admire any other. Not to cast aspersions on what you do—but acting—if I had my way, I would see a play every night.

HILEY: Or be in one.

ARIEL: That goes without saying.

HILEY: What time is your audition tomorrow?

ARIEL: (*He's beginning to know too much.*) ... 3:00 p.m.

HILEY: Then you'll be catching the 6:00 a.m. train. You are going to Kansas City aren't you—to audition?

ARIEL: I don't remember discussing this with you.

HILEY: You didn't.

ARIEL: You just knew?

(HILEY *nods*)

ARIEL: It's bad luck to even talk about it. (*She knocks on the wood of the work coffin.*) It's foolish to call it an audition. I don't consider myself a professional actress. Audition is a professional term.

HILEY: I've never seen you as anything but an actress. You have a wonderful carriage. You're a pleasure to watch.

ARIEL: (*Surprised*) Thank you.

HILEY: (*Smiling*) You're welcome.

ARIEL: First time I've heard that. I've been auditioning for a while now—fifteen years. And in all that time no one has said, "Thank you Miss Bright. You're a pleasure to watch."

HILEY: Not even a thank you.

(ARIEL *shakes her head.*)

That's rude.

ARIEL: Not rude. Rude means uncouth, uncultivated, un-polished. The Royal Kansas City Shakespeare Touring

Company is anything but that. Are you familiar with their work?

HILEY: No, but I'll be sure to acquaint myself when you join their company. (*Afraid he has said too much, he begins to scout about the room for something.*) There's a wonderful bottle of nail paste hiding somewhere.

(ARIEL *spots the jar on the desk and picks it up.*)

ARIEL: Looking for this?

HILEY: Yes.

ARIEL: (*Hands it to him.*) I thought it was a bottle of blood.

HILEY: Blood isn't really this color.

ARIEL: Nail paste matches the dress.

HILEY: That's why I bought it.

ARIEL: Sure you want to color her nails?

(HILEY *is coloring Mrs. Moxem's nails*)

HILEY: Yes.

ARIEL: I don't believe Mrs. Moxem wore nail paste.

HILEY: She didn't. But that doesn't mean she didn't want to.

ARIEL: (*Cautiously*) If someone asks where I am tomorrow—not that they will—but you will keep it a secret.

HILEY: If you like.

ARIEL: Good. Those kids I teach have teased me before. And their parents don't care for me either. One child reported that her mother said, "Enid Sneed gives herself airs." When she said that I felt like hiding.

(HILEY *is standing on his toes, trying to reach something on the top shelf.*)

ARIEL: What do you need?

HILEY: Emery board. I don't know why I put it up so high.

ARIEL: I don't know how you got it up there. (*She hands it to him.*)

HILEY: You are tall.

ARIEL: Grotesquely tall?

HILEY: No.

ARIEL: Without shoes I'm six-foot-one.

HILEY: (*Impressed*) That's tall.

ARIEL: (*Not pleased at all.*) For a thespian it's unheard of. Actors are the tiniest human beings I've ever seen. And they don't grow. Actor managers are even shorter and they're the ones who do the hiring. Mr. Madox, he's the manager I hate the most and last summer I was so tired of being turned down I said to him, "I could pick you up and drop you and from the height you'd be falling from it would hurt!" He's dead now.

ARIEL and HILEY: (*Simultaneously*) Trolley car.

ARIEL: A great actor—but a rotten pedestrian.

HILEY: Maybe someone taller took his place.

ARIEL: I doubt it.

HILEY: Seems to me ... yes, I remember reading about his replacement. Frank Ramsay. Isn't he the new actor manager for the Royal Kansas City Shakespeare Touring Company?

ARIEL: ...Yes.

HILEY: Said in the article he was real tall.

ARIEL: It did not.

HILEY: Did too. Didn't you read that article?

ARIEL: No and you didn't either.

HILEY: Guess you don't subscribe to the *Mortician Observer*.

ARIEL: There's no such paper. And you didn't read any article about Frank Ramsay being tall. Besides, even if he is tall, that doesn't mean he's going to hire tall people.

HILEY: But if he's six-foot-three, his leading lady could be six-foot-one or six-foot-two if she wore shoes.

ARIEL: That is, if he's six-foot-three.

HILEY: He is.

ARIEL: Don't say things like that to me, Hiley. I don't want to know.

HILEY: Of course you don't. Mind handing me the cold cream.

(*She brings it to him.*)

ARIEL: Getting ready to do the face?

HILEY: It won't be easy. She wants to look a certain way.

(HILEY *has laid the cosmetics out on the table.* ARIEL *begins to peruse through them and there are quite a lot to peruse.*)

ARIEL: I see you have the complete Lady Beechum collection. Heavens, look at all this. If I used cosmetics, which I don't, I would purchase Lady Beechum. What a delightful liprouge. Lovely shade. Did you buy this at Norwood's?

HILEY: Yes.

ARIEL: Well, I must pay the drugstore a visit. Not to buy, just to try it on.

HILEY: You could try it on here.

ARIEL: It looks like you've used it before.

HILEY: I haven't worn it.

ARIEL: No, but you've applied it to the lips of others.

HILEY: Yes.

(*Not wishing to put it on, she still finds it difficult to put down.*)

ARIEL: May I put it on Mrs. Moxem?

HILEY: You'll have to touch her.

ARIEL: I know.

HILEY: Dead people give you the willies.

ARIEL: But cosmetics don't. I'll use this. And this. And ... oh, violet eye powder. May I use this too? No, no, it wouldn't be right for Mrs. Moxem.

HILEY: Sure it would. That's why I have it out.

ARIEL: I can't use everything.

HILEY: I would.

ARIEL: If I do, she might look a bit brash.

HILEY: That's fine.

ARIEL: This is a woman who taught Bible classes.

HILEY: I know. (*To Mrs. Moxem*) I attended them. (*To ARIEL*) Be generous.

ARIEL: Well, all right. (*She begins to prepare the collection in the order it will be used, occasionally glancing at Mrs. Moxem to see if her choice is appropriate.*)

"Her vestal livery is but sick and green
And none but fools do wear it, cast it off.
It is my lady, O it is my love.
O that she knew she were.
She speaks, yet she says nothing: what of that?
Her eye discourses. I will answer it. (*Tries to dab powder on
    Mrs. Moxem's eye lid.*)
I am too bold." (*Pulls back*)

ARIEL: I don't think I can touch her. (*Dying to put the make-up on, she overcomes her fear.*) I did.

(HILEY *is busy arranging flowers. He takes the vase and heads for the parlor.*)

Hiley, don't go away ...

HILEY: I'm just going to bring these flowers out front. I'll be back. Mrs. Moxem, you behave yourself. (*To* ARIEL) She has a tendency to squirm around. (*He disappears behind the curtain.*)

ARIEL: Hiley! (*Touching the body with caution.*) I'm going to apply just a touch more of this. (*With more confidence now.*) A bit more of that. (*Truly enjoying herself*) And as much eye powder as your lids can hold. Before I'm through you are going to look better than Julia Marlowe. Everyone says she's so striking—so professional ... (*Sing-song voice*) But she talks like this ... And she sweeps at the air with her arms ... (ARIEL'S *arms sweep at the air.*) ... I saw her do *Much Ado About Nothing* and that's exactly what it was.

(HILEY *returns with a small satchel in his hand.*)

HILEY: Don't get carried away. Remember, you have a train to catch.

ARIEL: The 6:15.

HILEY: The 6:00 a.m.

ARIEL: That's right.

HILEY: How long are you planning to stay in Kansas City?

ARIEL: Well, if I'm hired, I'll tour the country. We'll head west first and then we'll move south and from there we'll travel to New York City. ... By the time we return to Missouri—that could be a year from now. And I might not even come back to Missouri. I might go on to Europe instead.

HILEY: You certainly travel light for a person doing so much traveling. Is this your suitcase?

(*She nods and crosses to him, taking the bag and placing it on the desk.*)

ARIEL: Thank you. I didn't want to leave it behind.

HILEY: Do you have things packed at home that you can send for if you get the job?

ARIEL: I suppose. I used to pack a suitcase, but I don't do that anymore.

HILEY: If you're hired, just send me a telegram and I'll rush over to that boarding house and pack up everything you have.

ARIEL: You are the sweetest man, Hiley, truly you are.

HILEY: Thank you.

ARIEL: But don't waste your day waiting for that telegram.

HILEY: Oh, I'll be here anyway.

ARIEL: But I can't say for sure that I'll attend the audition.

HILEY: Pardon?

ARIEL: I'm not saying I won't. I just can't envision being turned away again.

HILEY: This year you may not be.

ARIEL: I won't permit myself that thought—and for two weeks I haven't slept just for thinking about it. I don't know why I put myself through it anymore. It's not a pleasant experience. Last year they wouldn't even see me. I waited all day—waited all year for the opportunity to reacquaint them with my talent. I told a fib when I said I told Mr. Madox off.

HILEY: I know.

ARIEL: I would have picked him up and dropped him, but that man was so minuscule, I didn't even see him leave.

HILEY: Trolley car didn't see him either.

ARIEL: In fifteen summers I only met him once. He employed a lot of people who kept telling me I was wasting his time.

HILEY: Who says those people are working for Frank Ramsay?

ARIEL: Who says they aren't? People don't change.

HILEY: No one's forcing you to go to Kansas City.

ARIEL: I bought a train ticket but it can be refunded.

HILEY: Possibly.

ARIEL: What! Won't J.C. Ewalt give me my money back?

(HILEY *shrugs*)

ARIEL: Oh, he's like everyone else in Grayson. I wouldn't be a bit surprised if he did deny me my refund. Never has a town been populated by a greater collection of unkind, inconsiderate, small minded ...

HILEY: Not everyone fits that description.

(*Beat.* ARIEL *smiles.*)

ARIEL: No not everyone.

(*She catches his glance.* HILEY *breaks the mood.*)

HILEY: As I said, just let me know what you want packed.

ARIEL: Yes, Hiley.

HILEY: Do you have anything you'd like sent that isn't in your room? A pair of your shoes are at the repair shop, I believe.

ARIEL: I'll buy new shoes if I become a famous actress.

HILEY: Yes you will.

ARIEL: Buy new shoes, or become a famous actress?

HILEY: Pardon?

ARIEL: You aren't suggesting, are you that ...

HILEY: I didn't say anything. Now when you send that telegram, address it to Hileah Bedsal, not Hiley—That's just a nickname.

ARIEL: You act like I'm going to get the part.

(HILEY *smiles*)

What's so funny? ... I am going to get the part?

HILEY: I didn't say that.

ARIEL: Then what are you saying?

HILEY: I mustn't say.

ARIEL: Hiley!

HILEY: It's not as if you're going to die. If you were, I'd tell you whatever you wanted to know—just to give you a final pleasure. But ...

ARIEL: (*Cornering him*) It's not fair to hint at something and then not say it.

HILEY: You're right. It's wrong to hint and I have a tendency towards it, so I don't socialize much. But when I like someone the way I like you ... there's such a temptation. For instance ... (*Breaking away*)

ARIEL: Hiley!

HILEY: I met Claude Polmeir going into the post office and I could have saved him the trip by telling him, "You don't have any mail." But I didn't. I let him go right on in and find out for himself.

ARIEL: I'm not going to get the part.

HILEY: No, no ... that's not what I said.

ARIEL: Then say what you are trying to say.

HILEY: I can't tell you what it is.

ARIEL: You mean, you refuse.

HILEY: I refuse.

ARIEL: If you don't tell me ... (*She spots a bottle on the shelf and grabs it.*) If you don't tell me, I'm going to drink this bottle of embalming fluid.

HILEY: Ariel, don't!

ARIEL: "Eyes look your last!
  Arms, take your last embrace! And, lips, O you
  The doors of breath, seal with a righteous kiss
  A dateless bargain to engrossing death!"

(*She throws her head back—ready to drink.*)

HILEY: You'll get the part!

ARIEL: What?

HILEY: Frank Ramsay will hire you.

ARIEL: Oh my, Oh my ... Hiley!

(*She rushes to embrace him. He wraps his arms around her. She lets go.*)

ARIEL: Did I hurt you?

HILEY: No.

ARIEL: This is the most wonderful thing that's ever happened to me.

HILEY: That will happen to you.

ARIEL: And it will happen?

HILEY: Yes.

ARIEL: I'll be part of the company? Playing all sorts of roles?

HILEY: Oh yes.

ARIEL: All the time?

HILEY: Shakespeare—every night of the week except Sunday.

ARIEL: Shakespeare?

HILEY: That's right.

(ARIEL *collapses on the stool.*)

What's wrong?

ARIEL: I've forgotten all my Shakespeare. Every last verse. I must have swallowed some of that embalming fluid. Not enough to kill me, just enough to totally destroy my mind.

HILEY: (*Checking the bottle*) You couldn't have. The cap was on.

ARIEL: (*Backing away*) Vapors ... vapors escape.

HILEY: (*Approaching her*) You better sit down.

ARIEL: Don't touch me! You've touched a dead person with those hands.

HILEY: So have you.

ARIEL: (*Furiously wiping her hands together*.) What part will he give me tomorrow?

HILEY: Lady Macbeth.

ARIEL: They're doing the Scottish play? Bad luck from day one. Lord help me.

HILEY: I don't know why you're getting so upset.

ARIEL: You don't know? You mean there's finally something you don't know?

HILEY: I wish I'd kept my mouth shut. (*Returns to Mrs. Moxem*.)

ARIEL: So do I.

HILEY: I just wanted to brighten your spirits.

ARIEL: It didn't work.

HILEY: I'm usually so good at it. Made Mrs. Moxem laugh tonight.

ARIEL: She was about to die. I have a long road of misery ahead and I truly regret knowing about it.

HILEY: But you'll be acting.

ARIEL: With those tiny little people. Scurrying about the stage. Getting in my way.

HILEY: Frank Ramsay's six-foot-three.

ARIEL: And the biggest idiot I'll ever meet. Choosing an amateur to play Lady Macbeth. Only an amateur would do such a thing. My high regard for the Royal Kansas City Shakespeare Touring Company has been put to rest — completely.

HILEY: I'm sorry to hear that.

ARIEL: So am I.

HILEY: You planning on missing that train?

ARIEL: What time is it?

HILEY: 5:29.

ARIEL: No time to pack.

HILEY: Sure there is.

ARIEL: They'll expect me to come with costumes. And I haven't any to speak of. I made a few over the years but they're starting to look peculiar.

HILEY: If you're low on clothes, I could lend you some. Really, I've got three dresses in this chest just gathering dust.

ARIEL: Doubt they'll fit.

HILEY: You could let out the hem.

ARIEL: Those dresses belong to dead people.

HILEY: Eventually, but not yet. I'm a whole year ahead in funeral plans.

ARIEL: That's sweet, Hiley—but I'll bring what I have. If I decide to go.

HILEY: Not much time to decide.

ARIEL: I'm aware of that. I have a great deal to think about. My teaching career, for one. I do get the summers off. That's not something you just throw away.

HILEY: And you'll work all the time as an actress.

ARIEL: (*Nonchalantly*) Oh?

HILEY: Yes ... all over the world. And when you're not working you'll be with friends. You'll have one of those saloons like Sarah Bernhardt has.

ARIEL: A salon?

HILEY: Just jammed with interesting people. Painters, sculptors, dancers, writers—lounging on your furniture, eating your food—talking to you night and day. My, what a whirlwind you'll be part of.

ARIEL: They'll all be famous?

HILEY: So will you.

ARIEL: Heavens.

(HILEY *rushes to her*)

HILEY: What?

ARIEL: I think I'm going to be sick.

(*He walks her to a chair and kneels next to her.*)

HILEY: Hold my hand now. Yes, just relax. You've had a terrible shock. It's not every day a person learns they don't have to be unhappy.

ARIEL: You do have a soothing touch. I bet you're a marvelous mortician.

HILEY: (*Gently*) I'm the best.

(ARIEL *stares at him for a moment too long.*)

Ariel, you all right?

ARIEL: (*She's not*) Yes, I'm fine.

HILEY: Sure?

ARIEL: I just had a flash of something.

HILEY: (*Concerned*) Pain?

ARIEL: No. It's not that. Never mind. I'll be fine.

HILEY: Feel well enough to travel?

ARIEL: I guess.

HILEY: Well, time's awaiting, lady fair.

ARIEL: I know. I just had a flash that if I stayed ...

HILEY: (*Abruptly*) Yes, well, can't think about that.

ARIEL: But I am. I know what would happen.

HILEY: So do I.

ARIEL: And you still want me to leave?

HILEY: (*No*) Yes.

ARIEL: Would I make you that miserable?

HILEY: I'm not the one who'd be miserable.

ARIEL: Oh.

HILEY: It's really for the best.

ARIEL: I suppose ... It is a shame.

HILEY: I know. I've thought about it often.

ARIEL: You have?

HILEY: Yes.

ARIEL: I don't have to leave.

HILEY: No you don't.

ARIEL: Tell me what to do.

HILEY: You decide.

(*Beat. They kiss.*)

You are indeed a pleasure, Miss Ariel Bright.

(*She turns to him and smiles. She starts to get up.* HILEY *extends his hand to help her.*)

ARIEL: Thank you. (*Gently, she lets go of his hand and crosses to the desk.*) What time is it getting to be? ... It will take me five minutes to get to the boarding house. Fifteen to throw something in the suitcase. Should I take time out to wash my face? Does it look like I've been emotional?

HILEY: No ...

ARIEL: How much time does that leave me to get to the train?

HILEY: I'll drive you in the hearse. There's room to lie down in the back if you start feeling sick again.

ARIEL: What about Mrs. Moxem? Is it all right to leave her here?

HILEY: Do you want to bring her along?

ARIEL: Do we have to?

HILEY: No, I'll pack her in ice.

(HILEY *exits through the curtain.* ARIEL *calls after him.*)

ARIEL: How long will that take?

HILEY: (*Calling back*) No time at all.

(*He returns with a pair of earmuffs, a scarf, and a bucket of ice.* ARIEL *watches as he begins assembling Mrs. Moxem in a winter wardrobe.*)

ARIEL: Do you want me to go on ahead?

HILEY: No. I'll drive you over as soon as I'm done.

ARIEL: Would you like me to crank up the hearse?

HILEY: No, I'm the only one who can get her to start. She was working earlier today. That's a good sign.

ARIEL: Maybe you shouldn't drive me then.

(*Now that Mrs. Moxem is warmly dressed,* HILEY *gently pours ice about her.*)

HILEY: I'll get you there. (*Beat*) Train's running a little late. Ran into a snag up in Rushville. (*Beat*) Six-minute delay.

(*He turns to* ARIEL *who smiles. He begins to search his pockets.*)

Pocket money. Pocket money. You're going to forget your purse.

ARIEL: (*Holding her satchel*) No I won't. Now that I've been reminded.

(*Unable to find any pocket money of his own,* HILEY *grabs a wad of bills from the bust of the dress dummy.*)

HILEY: Just in case.

(HILEY *stuffs the money in his pants' pocket and then crosses to the hat rack to get his morning coat.* ARIEL *puts her satchel down, in order to help him on with his coat, and in doing so forgets to pick it up again. She heads for the curtain. He follows. She stops.*)

ARIEL: Wonderful dress.

HILEY: (*Admiring it as well.*) So you do like it.

ARIEL: Never said I didn't.

HILEY: You think it will make her look like a tart?

ARIEL: Absolutely.

HILEY: Good. (*He smiles at Mrs. Moxem.*) That's what she wanted to be.

(*He puts on his mortician's hat, with the long black ribbons that trail past his shoulders. The first few bars of "What A Friend We Have In Jesus" softly plays to a ragtime beat. He quickly surveys the room with his eyes, turns and then follows* ARIEL *through the curtain.*)

FADE

Furniture and Set Pieces

Desk, desk chair
Small red rug
Hatrack
Trunk
Writing table
Large blue rug
Half coffin
2 platforms (1-3 x 8; 1-4 x 8)
Basket of flowers
Potted palm
Straightback chair
Bookshelf
Dress dummy

Large red rug
Coffin with sliding tray
Cart
Stool
Tombstone (Inscription: "Mary Louise Moxem, Born August 6, 1813; died August 6, 1912")
2 pieces of burlap
2 pieces of crate sides
Low black box and thin stage weight to prop up end of half coffin, which is off platform)

Prop List

Jar of red nail paste
Hand mirror
3 business cards
Wood file box with "Ariel Bright" statictics cards, and "Seevers-Sinclair-Sleeper" cards
Desk lamp
Green vase of flowers
Red dress (on dummy)
Wad of bills
Jar of cold cream ("Lady Beechum")
Clear glass jar with emery boards
2 makeup brushes
2 tins blue eyeshadow; 1 tin violet eyeshadow; 1 tin dark

pink liprouge; 1 tin grey eyeshadow; 1 large tin of red eyeshadow; 1 small bottle of white makeup (all marked "Lady Beechum's")
Bottle of embalming fluid, capped (w/label; fluid inside is water)
1 beige round tube of Stein's
2 haircombs; 1 hairbrush
2 white rags; 1 white cloth with yellow stripe; 1 chamois cloth
For the pyramid card trick: 8 of hearts from a deck of large, patterned cards; one small patterned deck of cards
Mrs. Moxem: Wig head with

2 pieces grey hair attached; body shape covered by white sheet, feet sticking up
Plastic cloth: taped over Moxem to catch ice
Bucket, ice (approx. 5 lbs. per show)
Handbag with small oriental purse with ARIEL'S gloves, train ticket
Earmuffs, knit scarf
Pocket watch with chain (for HILEY)
Small pillow, for ARIEL'S head on half coffin
Black fabric (on half coffin floor, to protect costume)
Overhead light with green metal shade and pullchain
Pair of suspenders, black umbrella, grey sweater vest—all on hatrack
3 brown bottles on writing table
On desk: typewriter, box of collars, white feather, wooden cigar box, 2 hardback books, 1 small soft-covered book, 1 pamphlet, 1 bottle of ink, 1 pen with nib, penstand, round "Lady Beechum" jar
White shawl (on back of chair)
Green fabric remnant (on seat of chair)
Buttons, piece of lace (on cart)
Sliding tray
Green (painted) metal box, with white interior (trunk)
On bookshelf: clock without a face; many bottles; many small makeup tins

Costumes

Red dress for dress dummy

HILEY:
Black pinstripe pants; suspenders; white shirt; collar; cufflinks and studs; black vest with pockets; black coat; black top hat with ribbons; white apron with 2 pockets; black hightop shoes; wire-rimmed glasses; pocket watch with chain

ARIEL:
Corset; white hightop lace-up shoes; dress: skirt (white), bodice (white), jacket (white; flower on left breast of jacket); handkerchief; gloves (net; preset as a prop); large straw hat with white netting; white stockings; white garter; camisole

CHRONOLOGY OF MAJOR PRODUCTIONS,
1972–1985

1972–1973

Please Be Kind—Frank D. Gilroy
'Twas Brillig—Frank D. Gilroy
Present Tense—Frank D. Gilroy
Come Next Tuesday—Frank D. Gilroy
Three from Jimmy Ray's—John Ford Noonan, William Devane, Angelo Gnazzo

Summer 1973
Vermont

Actors—Conrad Bromberg
Mimosa Pudica—Curt Dempster
The Current Rage—Carol Roper

1973–1974

Studs Edsel—Percy Granger
Lost Jazz—John Ford Noonan
Michigan South and Mimosa Pudica—Curt Dempster
Actors and At Home—Conrad Bromberg

Summer 1974
Vermont Summer Theatre Festival
Where Do We Go From Here?—John Ford Noonan
The Dog Ran Away—Brother Jonathan Ringkamp, O.S.F.
Parades Shall Follow—Gary Nebiol and Don Marcus

1974–1975

Parades Shall Follow—Gary Nebiol and Don Marcus
The Dog Ran Away—Brother Jonathan Ringkamp, O.S.F.
Amnesia—Michael Shaffer
The Transfiguration of Benno Blimpie—Albert Innaurato

1975–1976
The Shortchanged Review—Michael Moody
Getting Through the Night—John Ford Noonan
Possession—Lyle Kessler
Money—Arthur Giron
Dreams of a Blacklisted Actor—Conrad Bromberg

1976–1977
The Contest—Shirley Lauro
Good-by and Keep Cold—John Ford Noonan
An Evening with Two Actresses—Barbara Tarbuck and Susan Merson
The Soft Touch—Neil Cuthbert

Special Evenings
Want—Arthur Morey
Innocent Pleasures—Arthur Giron
Eulogy for a Small-Time Thief—Miguel Pinero

1977–1978
Reflections of a China Doll—Susan Merson
Eulogy for a Small-Time Thief—Miguel Pinero
Innocent Pleasures—Arthur Giron
Mama Sang the Blues—Katherine Cortez

Marathon '78
First Annual Festival of One-Act Plays
The Daughter of Her Country—Vincent Canby
Buddy Pals—Neil Cuthbert
Pieces—Bill Cwikowski
Waiting for Mickey and Ava—Irene Dailey
Déjà Vu—Curt Dempster
The Next Contestant—Frank D. Gilroy
A Qualification for Anabiosis—Charles Gordone
Leaving Home—Marcia Haufrecht
Bicycle Boys—Peter Maloney
Playing Dolls—Susan Nanus
Those Summer Nights When the Dark Comes Late—John Ford Noonan

Blackout—Martin Sherman
Last Rite for Snow White—Robin Wagner
Split—Michael Weller
Auntie Hamlet—Dan Isaac
A Traveling Companion—Anthony McKay
Dotty the Dribblin' Droolin' Dame—Dimo Condos
From Whom It May Concern—Conrad Bromberg
Caveat Emptor—Betta Shaffran

1978–1979

End of the War—Vincent Canby
Three:
   Bicycle Boys—Peter Maloney
   Playing Dolls—Susan Nanus
   Buddy Pals—Neil Cuthbert
A Special Evening:
   The Old Tune—Robert Pinget
   The Man with the Flower in His Mouth—Luigi Pirandello
   Welfare—Marcia Haufrecht

New Voices
A Series of Staged Readings of New American Plays

Nesting—Chris Ceraso
The Ice Farm—Peter Maeck
New Mexico Rainbow Fishing—Jerry Stubblefield
What's So Beautiful About a Sunset Over Prarie Avenue?—Edward
  Allan Baker

Marathon '79

Vivien—Percy Granger
Dreams of Glory—Frank D. Gilroy
Irish Coffee—M.Z. Ribalow
The Coal Diamond—Shirley Lauro
Crossing the Crab Nebula—Lewis Black
Lost and Found—Peter Maloney
First Thirty—Neil Cuthbert
The Only Son—Curt Dempster
Unseen Friends—Katharine Long
George and Rosemary—Robin Wagner

Lucky Star—Marcia Haufrecht
Touch Black—Bill Bozzone

1979–1980

The Perfect Stranger—Neil Cuthbert
What's So Beautiful About a Sunset Over Prarie Avenue?—Edward
Allan Baker

THE INVENTATIONAL
A Festival of One-Act Plays

SERIES I:
The Pushcart Pedlars—Murray Schisgal
Tennessee—Romulus Linney

SERIES II:
Life Boat Drill—Tennessee Williams
Shoeshine—David Mamet
The Laundromat—Marsha Norman
Sister Mary Ignatius Explains It All For You—Christopher
  Durang

Marathon '80

Landscape with Waitress—Robert Pine
Bella Figura—Brother Jonathan Ringkemp, O.S.F.
On the Fritz—Lewis Black
An Arrangement of Convenience—Rosemary Toohey
Two-Part Harmony—Katharine Long
El Hermano—Romulus Linney
Sittin'—Chris Ceraso
The Store—Marcia Haufrecht

1980–1981

Father Dreams—Mary Gallagher
The Scented Garden—Tim Kelly
Geography of a Horse Dreamer (extended workshop)—Sam
  Shepard

Three from the Marathon

Two-Part Harmony—Katharine Long

El Hermano—Romulus Linney
Landscape with Waitress—Robert Pine

Marathon '81
*The Sermon*David Mamet
Stuck in the Pictures on a Sunday Afternoon—Bill Bozzone
A Public Street Marriage—Edward Allan Baker
The Lady or the Tiger—Shel Silverstein
In Cohoots—James Ryan
Down the Tubes—Brian McConnachie
April Offering—Elizabeth Karp
The Rodeo Stays in Town for at Least a Week—Jerry Stubblefield
The Smash—Neil Cuthbert
Dumping Ground—Elizabeth Diggs
Good Help Is Hard to Find—Arthur Kopit
Open Admissions—Shirley Lauro
American Garage—Peter Maloney

1981–1982
Best of the Marathon
The Sermon—David Mamet
Dumping Ground—Elizabeth Diggs
Open Admissions—Shirley Lauro
The Lady or the Tiger—Shel Silverstein
The House Across Street—Darrah Cloud
Bella Figura—Brother Jonathan Ringkamp, O.S.F.

New Voices
A Series of Staged Readings of New American Plays
Lily Dale—Horton Foote
Grunts—Joshua Brand
Dancers—Brendan Ward
Motherless Child—Rosemary McLaughlin
The Brass Bell Superette—Bill Bozzone

Marathon '82
The Forest Lawn Diet—Jim Richardson
Appearances—Tina Howe
The Fortress of Solitude—Jeffrey Jones

The Fisher Wedding—Carol Hall
The Self-Begotten—John Wellman
Fog—Conrad Bromberg
Goodbye, Howard—Romulus Linney
The Undefeated Rhumba Champ—Charles Leipart
Rosario and the Gypsies—Eduardo Machado
Class Reunion—Kermit Frazier
Kilo—Marc Berman
Many Happy Returns—Willie Reale
Routed—Jeffrey Sweet
Ord-Way Ames-Gay—Susan Vick
Buddies—Mary Gallagher

Octoberfest '81

(First annual month-long Festival of member-initiated projects; 26 projects done)

1982–1983

Welcome to the Moon—John Patrick Shanley

The Modern Ladies of Guanabacoa—Eduardo Machado

The House of Ramon Iglesia—Jose Rivera

New Voices

Series of Staged Readings of New American Plays
The Old Flag—Vincent Canby
To Gillian on Her 37th Birthday—Michael Brady
The Mud Angel—Darrah Cloud
E.Q.V.—Eric Conger
Terrain—Cassandra Medley

Octoberfest '82

(Month-long festival of member-initiated projects; 42 projects done)

Marathon '83

Five Unrelated Pieces—David Mamet
Touch Black—Bill Bozzone
The Dolphin Position—Percy Granger

Fast Women—Willie Reale
Two Hot Dogs with Everything—William Wise
Delusions of a Government Witness—Louis Lippa
Poisoner of the Wells—Brother Jonathan Ringkamp, O.S.F.
Cash—Stuart Spencer
Pastorale—Peter Maloney
Postcards—Carol Mack
Eulogy—Jim Richardson
Tender Offer—Wendy Wasserstein
The Survivalist—Robert Schenkkan
I Love You, I Love Not—Wendy Kesselman

1983–1984
To Gillian on Her 37th Birthday—Michael Brady
Broken Eggs—Eduardo Machado

New Voices
Staged Readings of New American Plays
Wild Milk—Darrah Cloud
Men Act, Women Talk—Guavanina
Landmarks—D.B. Gilles
The Bloodletters—Richard Greenberg
Androscoggin Fugue—Dick Beebe

Octoberfest '83
(Month-long Festival of member-initiated projects; 50 projects done)

Marathon '84
House—Danny Cahill
Remember Crazy Zelda?—Shel Silverstein
Bite the Hand—Ara Watson
Blood Bond—Gina Barnett
At Home—Richard Dresser
Fine Line—Janice Van Horne
Slam—Jane Willis
Jazz—Elizabeth Albrecht
Been Taken—Roger Hedden
A Sense of Loss—Mark Malone

Vermont Sketches—David Mamet
Saxophone Music—Bill Bozzone
Ariel Bright—Katharine Long
Raving—Paul Rudnick

1984-1985

The Bloodletters—Richard Greenberg
Once on a Summer's Day—Book and Lyrics by Art Perlman;
   Music by Jeffrey Lunden
The Crate—Shel Silverstein

New Voices

Series of Staged Readings of New American Plays

Dennis—James Ryan

Permission from Children—Kathleen Cahill

Small Corners—Randee Nguyen

Off in the Woods—Bill Bozzone

Been Taken—Roger Hedden

Octoberfest '85

(Month-long Festival of member-initiated projects; 66 projects done)

Life Under Water—Richard Greenberg
Mariens Kammer—Roger Hedden
The Frog Prince—David Mamet
Men Without Dates—Jane Willis
The Road to the Graveyard—Horton Foote
Aggressive Behavior—Stuart Spencer
Between Cars—Alan Zweibel
North of Providence—Edward Allan Baker
The Semi-formal—Louisa Jerauld
Painting a Wall—David Lan
One Tennis Shoe—Shel Silverstein

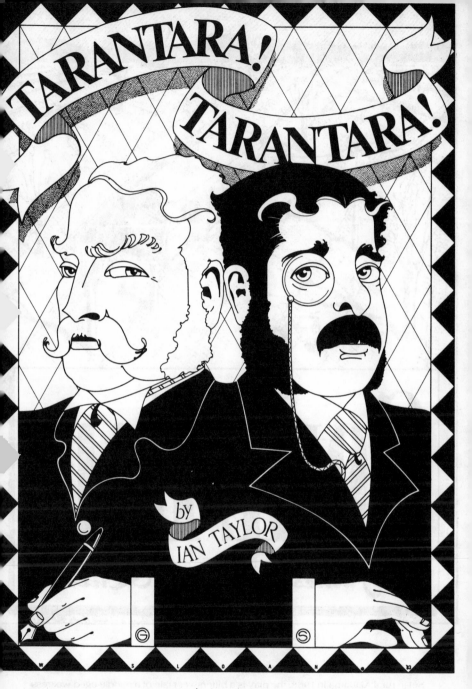

This delightful small scale musical is about the life of Gilbert and Sullivan. It is interspersed with some of the best known songs from the Savoy operas, including THE PIRATES OF PENZANCE, HMS PINAFORE and THE MIKADO. This show had a very successful run on the West End of London in 1975. Five males, three females, though more actors may be used as "stage-hands" and chorus members. Settings may be fluid and simple, or complex. A piano vocal score is available for perusal

SOME RAIN

by James Edward Luczak

Set in rural Alabama in 1968, the play is a bittersweet tale of a middle-aged waitress whose ability to love and be loved is re-kindled by her chance encounter with a young drifter. Two males, one female; single interior and exterior set.

ESCOFFIER
KING OF CHEFS
by
Owen S. Rackleff

©Tom V.H.

In this one-man show set in a Monte Carlo villa at the end of the last century, the grand master of the kitchen, Escoffier, ponders a glorious return from retirement. In doing so, he relates anecdotes about the famous and shares his mouth-watering recipes with the audience. One male; single interior set.

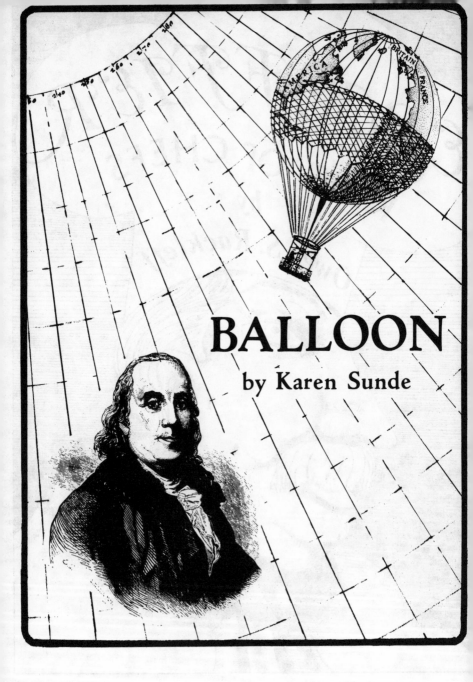

BALLOON

by Karen Sunde

18th century Paris is the setting of this structurally inventive play about Benjamin
Franklin and his French contemporaries. Five males, one female; single interior set.

LOOKING-GLASS

by Michael Sutton and Cynthia Mandelberg

This provocative chronicle, interspersed with fantasy sequences from ALICE IN
WONDERLAND, traces the career of Charles Dodgson (better known as Lewis Car-
roll) from his first work on the immortal classic, to his near downfall when accused
of immorality. Six males, four females with some doubling; either simple fluid staging
or elaborate sets can be used.

DEATH in the POT

by Manuel Van Loggem

An English style thriller with a fascinating plot that takes intricate twists and turns, as a husband and wife try to kill each other off, aided by a mysterious Merchant of Death. Four males, two females; single interior set.

A charming musical adaptation of Shakespeare's A MIDSUMMER NIGHT'S DREAM. This is one of the three shows written by the man who gave us LITTLE MARY SUNSHINE. Five males, three females, expandable with the use of a chorus; single exterior set. A piano score is available for perusal or rental.